The Homicide of Yafeu 'Yaki Kadafi' Fula

compiled by Yaasmyn Fula

ISBN 978-1733140027 (paperback); 978-1733140034 (e-book)

Front cover photo from collection of Yaasmyn Fula; one of four photographs found in Yaki's pocket during his autopsy.

Back cover photo by Yaasmyn Fula

Layout and cover design by Lily J. Noonan

Bearded Dragon Productions
Los Angeles, California

spiritofanoutlaw.com

When I die, bury me a G,
Open casket on them bastards
so they all remember me...
with my vest on my chest...
THUG LIFE

~ Yafeu "Yaki Kadafi" Fula
Lyrics from "Runnin'"
One Million Strong

Let the people see what they did to my boy.

The bullet went through Yaki's right eye and literally blew his brains out. The funeral director at Martin Funeral Home in Montclair, NJ was not sure if he could guarantee fixing his face to accommodate an open casket and asked me to consider a closed casket service. My beautiful baby boy.

I remember thinking at that time about Mamie Till, Emmett Till's mother; I got strength from this woman. When the savage beasts of Mississippi kidnapped and killed her beloved 14-year-old boy, his body revealed he had been tortured. She was confronted with the same horrific decisions as me. Open casket or closed casket. How do I protect my son's dignity yet at the same time cry out my pain?

Mamie Till's words echoed in my heart that day as I sat alone in the office at Martin Funeral Home.

"Let the people see what they did to my boy."

I told the funeral director, "Yes, it will be an open casket. It is what Yaki would have wanted."

The tears burned on my face. My brain was rejecting what I was seeing, as the scene from *The Godfather* when Marlon Brando stood viewing his dead son's body on the slab, "Look how they massacred my boy..." flashed before me.

The funeral director understood the almost impossible task before him and he did his best.

I want the world to see what was done to my son and the truth which has been covered up. Let the world know the truth and determine who has been lying for 25 years and why.

This book is a compilation of the police reports, witness statements, and other evidence used in the investigation of the homicide of my son. The document scans within this book were provided to me by the various agencies involved in the investigation and prosecution.

~ Yaasmyn Fula

Publisher's notes:

Documents are presented in chronological order.

All documents within this book are reproduced exactly as Yaasmyn Fula received them with the exception of redactions for Social Security numbers as noted on each summary.

Throughout the reports and statements, misspellings of names are common.

PREFACE

It is without dispute that Rashad "Roddy" Clark had a difficult start in life. His mother passed away from complications due to AIDS in 1987 when he was eight years old and his father died of a heart attack a few years later. By his 15th birthday, he was already involved with the world of drugs and dealing and the court system.

In 1995, Amer-I-Can, a program established by football legend Jim Brown, gave young Rashad the skills and opportunity to get on the right path. Rashad was one of only eleven teens to make it all the way through the intensive three-month mentoring program. At the ceremony celebrating his accomplishment, he was interviewed by the Newark Star-Ledger and he said he was looking forward to school and making something out of his life.

Yet on the night of November 10, 1996, just over a year after he finished the Amer-I-Can program, Rashad had a gun in his hand and he killed Yafeu "Yaki Kadafi" Fula, my only child.

To whom much is given, much is expected.

Not one member of his family contacted me, sent condolences, or offered even a card of sympathy. This disregard towards me is astounding because we weren't strangers. Rashad's cousin Mutah Beale was a regular visitor to my home and played with Yaki when they were young boys. After the murder of his parents, Mutah lived with his grandmother and grandfather. There was always a house full of boys, no parents, just a grandfather and a grandmother struggling. Members of the community who knew of his tragedy willingly gave sustenance and support to his family. I took Mutah to the park, had him go bike riding with Yaki, picked him up to just hang out.

As Tupac's career was taking off, Yaki was in New York working with Tupac in the studio with their group Dramacydal. I would pick Mutah up at his grandmother's house, assure her I would take care of Mutah, and bring him home. I remember taking him by his hand to meet Tupac in the hotel in Manhattan. My acts of kindness were ultimately treated with contempt and shocking abject disrespect.

In his book *All God's Children: The Bosket Family and the American Tradition of Violence*, Fox Butterfield studies the life of Willie Bosket, considered to be the most violent criminal in New York. As a young boy, he wreaked havoc on the streets of Harlem to release his rage. By the age of fifteen, Willie had shot and killed two men on the Manhattan subway and claimed to have committed 2,000 crimes, 200 armed robberies and 25 stabbings.

Yet within the rage and chaos of his mind, Willie Bosket's IQ was near genius level. In tracing the life of the Bosket family, Fox Butterfield chronicles a culture of violence Willie inherited from his father, a convicted murderer, to his grandfather, then his great grandfather, all the way through the slaveowners of his family, who meted out unspeakable violence on his ancestors.

This is the legacy of violence America has passed on: generational slaughter rooted in the criminal enterprise of capitalism/slavery which dehumanizes its subjects who in turn internalize violence to only perpetrate it upon society.

The murder of Yaki shares in this horrendous plague of violence. The violence perpetrated upon Rashad and his family was passed on, normalized, and became a pattern of daily life. The murder of Yaki was not an accident. It was intentional, it was planned, and it was carried out by a boy, like Willie Bosket, who had no empathy for others, filled with rage and self-hatred with his own mother and father dead.

As I stated in my remarks to the court in September 1998 at sentencing of Rashad, the blood stains of my child's death are on the hands of not only the murderer but on America as well for creating and perpetuating a climate of violence for decades that spawned this boy and taught him at an early age that fear and violence are normal.

The sickness of America plays out daily. The daily anguish of mothers losing their sons and daughters to police violence, racist violence, drug violence, domestic violence, generational violence.

I salute Ahmaud Arbery's family for having the fortitude to pursue and force the prosecution in Georgia to charge the killers with murder. In the case to find justice for my son, the killers were initially charged with Murder 1. But the glaring absence of family, community, and media support for Yaki's case - in addition to threats of violence against witnesses in 1996 - resulted in reduced charges and my ongoing solo quest for truth.

Contrary to what has been said for the past 25 years, this was not boys just playing with guns resulting in the death of one. That story is the myth created by those seeking to suppress the truth in order to protect their careers, pure public relations manufactured to maintain their status quo.

Also contrary to what you may have read or heard, ***there was no jury and there was no trial.*** Had there been, all of the evidence and statements contained herein would have been entered into the record during a trial.

However, I was told by investigators the witnesses were threatened and coerced and reluctant to testify in court. With the witnesses no longer willing to testify, the prosecutors decided they would not have a strong enough case to proceed at trial.

There was a plea deal for Rashad. The charge was changed from Murder 1 to Manslaughter 2 for this tragic sixteen-year-old, already a career criminal.

Charges against Kaseem Way, Rashad's accomplice, were dropped.

So the People are now the Jury and the Judges. The trial is now before the People of the World.

All Power to the People.

~ Yaasmyn Fula

ORANGE POLICE DEPARTMENT INCIDENT REPORT

Date: November 10, 1996
3 pages
Fax cover sheet not included. Redactions from providing agency.

Report states incident was at 325 Mechanic Street, 3rd floor.

Police respond to scene observing Yaki laying on his back shot in the head.

Police observe Lavie Johnson holding his left hand.

Lavie states Yaki was visiting from California and missed a plane earlier to go to Georgia.

Lavie states eight to ten minutes before the incident two black males knocked on her door and asked to speak with Yaki. A few minutes later she heard a gunshot.

Lavie states Yaki had been wearing a bulletproof vest because he had a lot of problems with people in the area because of his relationship with Tupac.

ORANGE P.D.

1) POLICE AGENCY

AGUIAR #70

INCIDENT REPORT

3) PREV. CC NO.

4) VICTIM OR OBJECT OF REPORT
FULA, YAFEU

5) RES. PHONE NO. UNK
6) BUS. PHONE NO. UNK
7) PAGE 1 of 3

8) ADDRESS OF VICTIM OR OBJECT OF REPORT
20 WHITTIER   E. ORANGE, N.J.

9) D.O.B. 10-9-87
9) APT. NO. —
10) FLOOR —

14) SOC. SEC # UNKNOWN

15) CRIME OR INCIDENT
AGG. ASSAULT WITH FIREARM

17) PERSON REPORTING CRIME OR INCIDENT
JOHNSON, CLAUDIA

18) RES PHONE NO 201-673-3617
19) BUS PHONE NO NONE

22) RESIDENCE OF PERSON REPORTING CRIME or INCIDENT
325 MECHANIC ST. 3RD FLOOR

23) LOCATION DISPATCHED TO
325 MECHANIC ST 3RD FLOOR

SECTOR # 112

24) TIME REPORTED
03:48 AM

25) DATE REPORTED
11/10/96

27) WAS FORCE USED
☒ YES ☐ NO ☐ UNKNOW

29) STRANGER TO STRANGER
☐ YES ☐ NO ☒ UNKNOWN

28) WAS WEAPON USED
☒ YES ☐ NO ☐ UNKNOW

30) HOW ATTACKED
SHOT

31) TYPE OF PREMISES
HALLWAY

32) OBJECT OF ATTACK
UNKNOWN FIRE ARM

33) MEANS OF ATTACK
UNKNOWN.

34) MODUS OPERANDI

35) VEHICLE INVOLVED IN CRIME or INCIDENT
☐ STOLEN ☐ USED by OFFENDER ☐ INVOLVED

36) YEAR
37) MAKE
38) MODEL
39) LIC. PLATE NO.
40) STATE

N/A

41) COLOR

42) SERIAL NO.
43) BODY TYPE

44) NAME OF SUBJECT OR MISSING PERSON STATE ALIAS IN BOX 59
45) RESIDENCE
46) SOCIAL SECURITY NO.

47) SEX | 48) RACE | 49) AGE | 49A) D.O.B | 49B) PLACE OF BIRTH | 50) HEIGHT (INCHES) | 51) WEIGHT | 52) HAIR | 53) EYES | 54) CLOTHING WORN AND PECULIARITIES

55) ADDITIONAL INFORMATION

ON ABOVE DATE AND TIME I RESPONDED TO 325 MECHANIC ST. ON
THIRD FLOOR WERE IT WAS REPORTED THAT A YOUNG BLACK MALE HAD
BEEN SHOT IN THE HEAD. I ENTERED THE THIRD FLOOR HALL WAY AND
OBSERVED A YOUNG BLACK MALE (#4) LAYING ON HIS BACK ON THE FLOOR
WITH BLOOD OVER THE RIGHT SIDE OF THE FACE. HOLDING HIS LEFT
HAND WAS A YOUNG BLACK GIRL LATER KNOWN AS MS. LAVIE JOHNSON
AND MRS. CLAUDIA JOHNSON. I ALSO OBSERVED A GREEN IN COLOR
PIPE APPROX. 2 FEET FROM THE VICTIMS FOOT. I THEN ASKED MS. LA

62) PERSON ARRESTED
63) ARREST NO.
64) PERSON ARRESTED
65) ARREST NO.

66) PERSON ARRESTED
67) ARREST NO.
68) PERSON ARRESTED
69) ARREST NO.

N/A

70) WITNESSES (NAME AND ADDRESS)
71) PHONE
72) TELETYPE
73) LOCAL NOTIFIED

DEATHS SUICIDES
76) MEDICAL EXAMINER NOTIFIED
77) BODY WAS   RELEASED BY PHONE / PICKED UP
78) PRONOUNCED DEAD BY:
FOR HRS.   AT

N/A

AUTO THEFTS
79) RECOVERED AT
80) TIME
81) DATE
82) CAR TAKEN TO
83) VEHICLE PICKED UP BY

N/A

84) REPORTING OFFICER(S) SIGNATURE
85) EMP. NO. 70
86) APPROVING SUPERVISORS SIGNATURE
87) EMP. NO.

ORANGE POLICE DEPT.
Incident Report Supplement

CC NO. **96-29039**
PREV. CC NO.

PAGE 2 OF 3

JOHNSON AND MRS. CLAUDIA JOHNSON TO ENTER THERE APARTMENT IN ORDER TO CONSERVE THE CRIME SCENE. MRS. CLAUDIA JOHNSON THEN ENTERED THE APARTMENT 310. AT THIS TIME OFF. B. TRUVATO, OFF. B. SMITH AND LT. T. SMITH ARRIVED ON SCENE. I THEN ENTERED APT 310 AND SPOKE TO MRS. CLAUDIA JOHNSON AND HER DAUGHTER LAVIE JOHNSON WHO THEN TOLD ME THAT THE VICTIM WAS A MR. YAFEN FULA WHICH WAS LAVIE JOHNSON'S BOYFRIEND AND THAT HE HAD BEEN VISITING FROM CALIFORNIA AND HAD MISSED A PLANE EARLIER TODAY GOING TO GEORGIA. MRS CLAUDIA JOHNSON THEN STATED THAT APPROX 8-10 MINUTES BEFORE THE INCIDENT OCCURED SHE HEARD SOMEONE KNOCK ON HER DOOR. UPON ANSWERING THE DOOR SHE WAS CONFRONTED BY 2 BLACK MALES ONE OF THEM BEING APPROX 5'5 IN HEIGHT, SLIM BUILD, LIGHT SKINNED, BROWN EYES WEARING A GREEN JACKET WITH DARK PANTS AND A SHAVED HAIRCUT WITH A SOLID BLACK OR DK. BLUE BASEBALL CAP. THE OTHER SUSPECT WAS APPROX. 5'2 IN HEIGHT, SLIM BUILT, BROWN EYES, BROWN HAIR, DARK SKINNED WEARING A BLACK SHIRT & BLUE JEANS AND A GREEN AND BLUE JACKET. BOTH SUSPECTS APPEARED TO BE 18 & 20 YEARS OF AGE. MRS. CLAUDIA JOHNSON STATES THAT THE UNKNOWN ACTORS ASKED TO SPEAK TO THE VICTIM. THE VICTIM THEN ANSWERED THE DOOR AND GREETED THE ACTORS AS IF THEY WERE FRIENDS. A FEW MINUTES LATER MRS. CLAUDIA AND LAVIE STATE THEY HEARD A GUN SHOT WHEN THEY LOOKED OUT THE DOOR THE SAW THE VICTIM ON THE FLOOR AND BOTH ACTORS HAD FLED. MRS. JOHNSON THEN NOTIFIED US. MS. LAVIE JOHNSON STATED THAT MR. FULA HAD BEEN WEARING

REPORTING OFFICER SIGNATURE   EMP. NO. 70   DATE 11/10/96   APPROVED SUPERVISOR'S SIGNATURE   EMP. NO. 534   DATE 11-10-96

ORANGE POLICE DEPT.
Incident Report Supplement

CE NO. 96-29039
PREV. CE NO.

Page 3 of 3

A BULLETPROOF VEST BECAUSE MR. FULA WAS THE BELATED RAP SINGER TUPAC'S BROTHER, AND THAT HE HAD ALOT OF PROBLEMS WITH PEOPLE IN THE AREA BECAUSE OF IT. I THEN ASKED MS. AND MRS. JOHNSON TO STAY IN THE APARTMENT AND THAT MR. FULA WOULD BE TRANSPORTED TO U.M.D HOSPITAL. I THEN EXITED THE APARTMENT AND OBSERVED EMS TREATING THE VICTIM AND ALL THE VICTIMS CLOTHING AND A WHITE COLORED BULLET PROOF VEST WERE PLACED TO THE SIDE BY E.M.S. LT. T. SMITH THEN TOLD ME TO FOLLOW THE EMS UNITS TO U.M.D HOSPITAL LOCATED AT 150 BERGEN STREET IN NEWARK FOR TREATMENT. UPON OUR ARRIVAL WE WERE MET BY DR. DAVID H. LIVINGSTON. I OBSERVED DR. LIVINGSTON TREATING THE VICTIM AND OBSERVED HIM PULL OUT ONE GLASS VILE WITH A TAN COLORED TOP CONTAINING A WHITE SUBSTANCE. I THEN ASSISTED THE NURSES WITH THE PATIENTS CLOTHING AND FOUND $61.30 IN U.S. CURRENCY, SOME PERSONAL PAPERS AND A SMALL ZIPLOC BAG WITH A GREEN VEGETATION OF ALLEGED MARIJUANA. THE VICTIMS CLOTHING AND PERSONAL VALUABLE WERE IN MY POSSESION UNTIL T.O.T DET. J. ANDERSON. DR. LIVINGSTON STATED THAT THE VICTIM SUSTAINED A BULLET TO THE UPPER RIGHT SIDE OF RIGHT EYE. DR. LIVINGSTON ALSO STATED THAT THE BULLET REMAINED IN THE VICTIMS HEAD AND THAT HE WAS GOING TO BE PLACED IN INTENSIVE CARE UNIT WITH A LIFE SUPPORT APPARATUS.

REPORTING OFFICER SIGNATURE | EMP. NO. 70 | DATE 11/10/96 | APPROVING SUPERVISOR SIGNATURE | EMP. NO. 534 | DATE 11-10-96

DEATH CERTIFICATE OF YAFEU A. FULA

Date of death: November 10, 1996
1 page
Social Security number redacted by publisher.

Date of death is November 10, 1996, at 1808.

Parents are Sekou Odinga and Yaasmyn Smith (maiden name).

Informed by Yaasmyn Fula, mother.

Cause of death is gunshot wound to head.

Cemetery is Glendale Cemetery, Bloomfield, New Jersey.

City of Newark, New Jersey
BUREAU OF VITAL RECORDS

This is to certify that the following is a true copy of an official Death Record maintained by the Bureau of Vital Statistics, City of Newark, N.J. Do not accept this certificate unless the raised seal of the Bureau is affixed hereon.

DN- 04738

New Jersey State Department of Health
CERTIFICATE OF DEATH

STATE USE ONLY

1 NAME OF DECEASED			
Yafeu	A.	Fula	

2 DATE OF DEATH	3 SEX	4 DATE OF BIRTH	5a AGE - Last Birth	5b UNDER YEAR	6 DATE OF DEATH
11-10-96	M	10-9-77	19		

7a PLACE OF DEATH HOSPITAL ☒ INPATIENT ☐ ER/OUTPATIENT ☐ DOA OTHER ☐ NURSING HOME ☐ RESIDENCE ☐ OTHER (Specify)

7b FACILITY NAME	7c CITY/TOWN OR LOCATION	8 COUNTY
UMDNJ	NEWARK	ESSEX

8a RESIDENCE STATE	8b COUNTY	8c CITY OR TOWN	8d STREET AND NUMBER	8e INSIDE CITY LIMITS	8f ZIP CODE
NJ	Essex	Orange	20 Whittier Street	☒ YES ☐ NO	07050

9 BIRTHPLACE	10a DECEDENT EVER IN U.S. ARMED FORCES?	10b MARITAL STATUS
New York, NY	☐ YES ☒ NO	☒ NEVER MARRIED ☐ WIDOWED ☐ MARRIED ☐ DIVORCED

12 SURVIVING SPOUSE | 13a USUAL OCCUPATION: Entertainer | 14 KIND OF BUSINESS OR INDUSTRY --

15 NAME AND ADDRESS OF LAST EMPLOYER
Euthanasia Production Company- Los Angeles, CA

16 RACE 1 ☐ WHITE 2 ☒ BLACK 3 ☐ AMER. INDIAN 4 ☐ OTHER (Specify)	17 OF HISPANIC ORIGIN? ☐ YES ☒ NO 1 ☐ MEXICAN 2 ☐ CUBAN 3 ☐ PUERTO RICAN 4 ☐ CENT./SO. AMERICA 5 ☐ OTHER (Specify)	18 DECEDENT'S EDUCATION 10 Yrs

19 NAME OF FATHER			20 MAIDEN NAME OF MOTHER	
Sekou	Odinga		Yaasmyn	Smith

21a NAME OF INFORMANT	21b RELATIONSHIP	22 DISPOSITION ☒ BURIAL ☐ CREMATION ☐ ENTOMBMENT ☐ OTHER (Specify)
Yaasmyn Fula	Mother	

23a NAME OF CEMETERY OR CREMATORY	23b CITY	23c STATE
Glendale Cemetery	Bloomfield	NJ

23a NAME AND ADDRESS OF FUNERAL HOME
Martin's Home for Service, Inc. 40 Elm Street Montclair, NJ 07042

25a SIGNATURE OF FUNERAL DIRECTOR	25c NJ LICENSE NO # 2515	SIGNATURE OF LOCAL REGISTRAR	25b DATE RECEIVED 11-13-96
Thomas C. Brown			

25c TIME OF DEATH 1808 M	25b DATE AND HOUR PRONOUNCED DEAD DATE 11-10-96 HOUR 1808 M	25b DATE SIGNED

Complete items 25c d only when certifying physician is not available at time of death to certify cause of death

25c TO THE BEST OF MY KNOWLEDGE, DEATH OCCURRED AT TIME, DATE AND PLACE INDICATED
SIGNATURE OF PRONOUNCER (if different than certifier)

26 PART I

	IMMEDIATE CAUSE (Final disease or condition resulting in death)	INTERVAL BETWEEN ONSET AND DEATH
a	GUNSHOT WOUND TO HEAD	

Sequentially list conditions, if any, leading to immediate cause. Enter UNDERLYING CAUSE (Disease or injury that initiated events resulting in death) LAST.

b	DUE TO OR AS A CONSEQUENCE OF
c	DUE TO OR AS A CONSEQUENCE OF
d	DUE TO OR AS A CONSEQUENCE OF

PART II Other significant conditions contributing to death but not related to underlying cause in PART I

27 IF FEMALE	28 WAS AN AUTOPSY PERFORMED?

29 DATE OF INJURY 11-10-96	30a TIME OF INJURY 0348 M	30b INJURY AT WORK ☐ YES ☒ NO	30d DESCRIBE HOW INJURY OCCURRED Subject shot by assailant by fire arm

30c PLACE ☒ HOME ☐ OFFICE BUILDING ☐ FARM ☐ FACTORY ☐ STREET ☐ OTHER (Specify)

30e CITY AND COUNTY		30f STATE
STREET ORANGE	ESSEX	NJ

JUNAID R. SHAIKH, M.D.
325 NORFOLK STREET
NEWARK, NJ 07103

☐ CERTIFYING PHYSICIAN ☒ MEDICAL EXAMINER ☐ PRONOUNCER AND CERTIFIER

SIGNATURE OF CERTIFIER	31c DATE SIGNED
Shaikh MD	11-11-96

In Witness Whereof, I have hereunto set my hand and affixed the seal of Bureau of Vital Statistics,

Newark, N.J., this ...... **3rd** ...... day of ...... **November** ...... A.D. 19 **99**

Done Royster, Dep. Registrar

(Registrar of Vital Statistics)

ESSEX CO. MEDICAL EXAMINER'S REPORT

Date: various, beginning November 10, 1996
12 pages
Social Security number redacted by publisher. Underlines and other notations from providing agency.

Cause of death: Gunshot wound to the head.

Manner of death: Homicide.

Wound to right eye and back of head.

Brain dead, Yaki was put on life support until his mother could arrive from California.

No shells, bullets, or weapons recovered at the scene.

Bullet was removed from Yaki's brain by the medical examiner.

A woman heard a gunshot in the hallway and found Yaki in the hallway alone with the two visitors gone.

Yaki was wearing a Kevlar bulletproof jacket.

Four photos of decedent were found in pocket of clothing.

Toxicology analysis requested.

County of _Essex_

Street Address _____ P O & Zip Code _____

CASE IDENTIFICATION NUMBER

County	Year	Seq	Number
07	96	23	01

REPORT OF INVESTIGATION BY MEDICAL EXAMINER

1 | Format/Record [ ]

Current Status of this Case
1 - Closed
2 - Pending Final Report [1]

Death Certificate
1 - Finalized
2 - Pending [1]

HOMICIDE

This is
1 - A New Report
2 - Update Inform [1]

C IDENTIFICATION OF DECEDENT

Last Name: **FULA**

First Name, Middle Initial: **YAFEU**

2 J

Street Address: **20 WHittier ST**

Post Office and State: **EAST ORANGE NJ**

Occupation: **Unemployed**

OCC Code: [ ]

AGE CODES
D - Days
H - Hours
M - Months
Y - Years

"E" OR Y / "A" [A]
Age: 0 1 9
Birth Date: Mo 1 0 Day 0 9 Year 7 7

Social Security Number: **0 0 0 4 4 4 5 B**

MARITAL STATUS
M - Married   S - Single
D - Divorced   W - Widowed
U - Unknown

[S]

RACE OR ETHNIC ORIGIN
W - White   B - Black   Y - Oriental
R - Red   H - Hispanic M - Mixed
O - Other   U - Unknown

Race [B]   Sex [M]

SYNOPSIS OF HISTORY: GSW wound right and Back of head

Copy of chart, CT scan, x-ray, Blood sample requested. Clothes and valuables taken By police officer Badge #70

NOK: Afiafam Fula - mother 213-954-9134

PMD:

3 D

EVENT	Month	Day	Year	Time (24 Hours)	By Whom	Title
MEDICAL EXAMINER NOTIFIED	11	10	96	1845	Dr. Oruwari 982-5757 UMDNJ Surgical Icu	MD

	Month	Day	Year	Time	By Whom	Relationship/Title
LAST SEEN ALIVE						

	Month	Day	Year	Time	Place	
INJURY OR ONSET OF ILLNESS/FOUND	11	10	96	PRIOR TO 0348	325 MECHANIC ST ORANGE 3RD FLOOR	

E

	Month	Day	Year	Time	By Whom	Where
DEATH PRONOUNCED	11	10	96	1808	DR ORUWARI	UMDNJ SICU

CC# 96-29034

	Month	Day	Year	Time	By Whom	
POLICE NOTIFIED	11	10	96	0348		

	Month	Day	Year	Time	By Whom	Title
BODY TRANSPORTED	11	10	96	0015	SUBURBAN REMOVAL SERVICES	LIVERY

5 F ACTION TAKEN

1 = Not M.E.
2 = Accepted [2]

	Month	Day	Year	Time	By Whom	Scene M.E. or M.I.
Released or Scene Examination	11	10	96	1852	Stokes	

Scene Photos By		Month	Day	Year	Time	Viewed By	
	VIEWING						

Location of Viewing:

Viewed Photos By:

Viewed
1 = With Studies
2 = Without

MEDICAL EXAMINER INVESTIGATIVE DATA SHEET

Decedent's Name: _Tula Yafee_   Case Number: _07 4u 2301_

Information taken by: _Stirer_ _____ _"/_/'/_   Time: _1452_

Source of information: _Dr. Onuware_   Relationship to decedent: _MD_

From what agency (if applicable): _UMD NJ S..u_

Address: _____   Town, State: _____

Main phone: _982 5757_   Contact # _____   Other phone: _____

Information: _Subj. arrived at E.R. at 0415 intubated c_
_signs of life. GSW __ right eye and Back of head. ACLS_
initiated in the field

    _Brain death __ initiated at 0500 Second Brain_
flow study completed at 1300 and pronouncement done.

    Subj's mother was in California and wanted subj. to
remain on life support until she arrived. She arrived and spent
approx 30 min. c subj. until 1800 when he went into CL Pub to
asystole.

    Copies of chart, CT scan, all tests requested, along c
pre-mortem Blood samples Clothes and valuables receipted to
_P.D._

    Incident location unknown, not on Ambulance run sheet, but
believed to be Newark.

    Subj's mother and family left and no known local phone
given.

    Bullet not recovered.

Investigator's Name (print): _MARilyn A. Stirey_

Investigator's signature: _Marilyn Stirei_

M.E. Initials: _____   Date: _____   page _1_ of

MEDICAL EXAMINER INVESTIGATIVE DATA SHEET

Decedent's Name: _Fula, Yafee_ Case Number: _07-96-2301_

Information taken by: _Storei_ Date: _11/10/96_ Time: _1715_

Source of information: _Newark PD_ Relationship to decedent: _____

From what agency (if applicable): _____

Address: _____ Town, State: _____

Main phone: _733-8886_ Contact phone: _____ Other phone: _____

Information: _Call placed to Lt. O'Connell, Newark PD, he'll have_
homicide det. call back.

1925- Det. Blue, Homicide will check and see if he can determine incident
location.
1936- call to UMD NJ ER - no info on incident location.
1944- Call to UMD NJ Still - requested by run sheet again - incident
location 375 Mechanic St., Orange
1943- call to Orange PD, 266-4111, Sgt. Eziekian, he will fax
PD report to RMEO and contact homicide to call RMEO.
1955 Inv. Howard Johnson, Essex Co. Prosecutors office, Homicide
notified.

Investigator's Name (print): _MARILYN A. Storei_

Investigator's signature: _Marilyn A Storei_

MEDICAL EXAMINER INVESTIGATIVE DATA SHEET

Decedent's Name: FULA, YAFEU   Case number: 07-96-2301

Information taken by: GARDNER   11-10-96   Time: 23:17

Source of information: DET. YOUNG   Relationship to decedent: DETECTIVE

From what agency (if applicable): ORANGE P.D.

Address: _____   Town, State: _____

Main phone: _____   Contact ph.: 201-266-4111   Other phone: _____

Information: Not the primary detective, has minimal information

Shooting in 3rd floor hallway of 325 Mechanic St., an Orange housing project building, 11/10/96 at approx. 03:48. Alleged events:

Subject was at the same address -- Det. Young does not know why. Two individuals exited an Irvington car and knock on door of 3rd floor apt. A woman -- Det. Young is not sure of relationship to subject -- answered and the individuals asked for subject, who went into the hallway to speak with them. The woman at some point later heard a gunshot, found subject in the hall with a GSW and the 2 individuals gone. No suspect(s) or weapon(s) in custody, no shell(s) or bullet(s) recovered. Det. Young does not know motive.

- M.I. requested that O.P.D. bring report and clothing to autopsy; advised Det. Young to have officer at M.E.O. by 09:30 unless otherwise informed.

_____

_____

_____

Investigator's Name (print): MAUREEN GARDNER

Investigator's signature: Maureen Gardner

M.E. Initials: _____   Date: _____   page 4 of ____

STATE OF NEW JERSEY
REGIONAL MEDICAL EXAMINER OFFICE
EDWIN H. ALBANO INSTITUTE OF FORENSIC SCIENCE
325 NORFOLK STREET
NEWARK, NEW JERSEY 07103-2701

Johnson

(201) 648-7259
(201) 648-3914

Counties of:
Essex, Hudson,
Passaic, and Somerset

07962301.AUT
YAFEU, FULA

CERTIFICATION:

This is to certify that I, Junaid R. Shaikh M.D., Associate Medical Examiner have conducted a postmortem examination and autopsy on the refrigerated body of Yafeu Fula at the Institute of Forensic Science in Newark, New Jersey on November 10, 1996 between 0935 hours and 1300 hours with the assistance of autopsy assistant, Davis Ferrer. The body was identified by mother Yaasmyn Fula. Present during the autopsy procedure was Detective Dunn of the Orange police department.

EXTERNAL EXAMINATION:

The body was that of a well developed, well nourished black light complected male that was received unclad. The body weighed 203 pounds was 76" in height and appeared compatible with the reported age of 19 years. The body was cold. Rigor was present and fixed to an equal degree in all extremities. Lividity was present and fixed on the posterior surface of the body except in areas exposed to pressure. The scalp hair was black, curly and pleated into seven braids that were tapered towards the nape into ponytails that measured upto 7" long. The deceased wore a mustache and had a short goatee. The left irides was brown and left cornea was clear. The left conjunctiva was unremarkable and the left sclera was white. The right eye was flaccid and dislodged from its socket with extensive hemorrhage in the entire right eyeglobe. Injury to the right orbital region will be mentioned below. The external auditory canals were free of foreign material and abnormal secretions. Blood was present in the oral cavity and external nares. The nasal septum was intact. The teeth were natural and in good condition. The neck revealed no evidence of significant injury. Superficial ecchymosis was noted in the lateral aspect of the left side of the neck measuring 1" this showed petechial hemorrhages in the center, similar and faintly visible ecchymotic area with central areas of petechial hemorrhages was noted in the right lateral neck measuring 3/4". The chest was unremarkable. No evidence of injury of the ribs or sternum was evident externally.

A large tattoo was present in the chest and upper abdomen, this depicted a cross with vertically inscribed "Thug Life" and across "Live it Up", "Give it Up", in the four corners of the cross were the following words "Death Honor Dis Before", below the cross was the inscription "We don't shed Tears we shed Blood, Still Wanna be A Thug".

The abdomen was flat. No injuries were identified. The fingernails were intact and were clean. No injuries to the lower extremities were identified, there was no fractures lacerations or deformities. Old non-descript scars were noted on both the knee regions. Two recent healing scars with scab were noted in the right shin region these measured upto 3/16". No needle tracks were observed on the extremities.

Tattoo of a word "Outlaw" was on the dorsal aspect of the left forearm. On the left arm in the deltoid region was a tattoo of a dragon with a machine gun and long belt of cartridges, inscription above this was "Lord Bless the Dead Rest in Peace Makaveli Don" and below this a tattoo of the Devil, inscribed below was "21 gun salute my black Jesus". On the lateral aspect of the right side of the neck was the tattoo of the word "Kadafi".

The external genitalia were that of a normal adult male. The penis was circumcised. The testes were in the scrotum and the scrotal skin was appropriately rugated and free of trauma. The posterior was without note.

EVIDENCE OF THERAPY:
A endotracheal tube was present in the left nostril. Vascular catheters was in both the antecubital fossa and in the medial aspect of the right antecubital fossa. Needle puncture marks were noted in the right wrist region. A orange candy striped hospital tag encircled the left wrist bearing #008336364 and #000444513-6315. A orange identification tag from our office encircled the left ankle. Accompanying in the bodybag was a red top 20 cc vacutainer containing decedent's blood with hospital #000444513-6315.

CLOTHING:
Brought in by Detective Dunn of the Orange Police Department were the alleged clothing of the deceased. These were examined and showed small amount of blood specially in the upper clothing, these had been scissor cut by emergency personnel.

1. Kevlar bullet proof jacket size 44 with the inner part of the jacket that was size 43.

2. Hydrotex, size 11 high-top black leather boots.

3. Ski cap, woolen, yellow colored.

4. Blue denim jeans make "Marc Brachanon-Pelle", size 40.

5. One white sock.

6. Brown belt.

7. Black long john top make "E. J. Morgan" size 54/56.

8. Black short sleeve T-shirt size XXL make "Polo Jeans Company Ralph Lauren", this garment had the flag logo in the front of the chest.

9. Blue silk short sleeve T-shirt, make "Genelli" 1X size.

10. Black short sleeve T-shirt, make "Gildean", size XL/TG. On the left sleeve was the logo "Makaveli" and on the front a logo showing people lifting weighs and the logo stating "Born Outlawz Live it or Give it Up".

11. Black windbreaker make "Echo Unlimited", 100% nylon size XXL.

Recovered from the right front pocket were 4 photo's of the decedent in various poses and in the left front pocket a receipt from a fast food restaurant.

The clothing were examined and returned to the officer.

EVIDENCE OF INJURY:
Located and just above the medial canthus of the right eye and on the upper eyelid was a entrance gunshot wound that measured 7/16" in diameter with a barely noticeable less than 1/16" abrasion rim. The highest point of the entrance gunshot wound was located 4" below the top of the head and 11/16" right of the anterior midline. The periorbital tissue around the right eye was markedly edematous and showed marked contusion. The right eyeglobe was flaccid and had almost enucleated. Stippling was noted in the nasal, right malar and upper forehead regions. This extended to a area that measured 5" horizontally and 4" vertically in its maximum.

The hemorrhagic wound track perforated the skin to enter the right eyesocket, perforated through the right lesser wing on the sphenoid bone to enter the right cerebral hemisphere in its inferior aspect, it went through the temporal lobe and terminated in the right parieto-occipital region. The bullet created a almost circular fracture in the right squamosal part of the temporal bone which measured approximately 1" in greatest dimension, this had outward bevelling. The highest point of this fracture was located 3" below the top of the head. Recovered in the brain substance just at the cortical rim was a deformed large caliber gray metal bullet that weighed 9.6 grams. Associated was extensive laceration of the right hemisphere of the brain extensive subarachnoid hemorrhage and subdural hemorrhage over the right cerebral hemisphere. Associated fractures including fracture extending from the squamosal suture of the right temporal bone into the right parietal bone and multiple fractures involving the sella turcica, the right orbital plate and the right temporal bone upto the lateral aspect of the right petrous bone and fracture extending from the posterior aspect of the petrous bone involving the right occipital bone. The trajectory was front to back towards the right and slightly upwards.

A circular contusion was noted in the maxillary part of the left cheek anteriorly measuring 3/4" x 1/4".

INTERNAL EXAMINATION:
BODY CAVITIES:
The body is opened by the usual Y-shaped thoraco-abdominal incision and the chest plate was removed. No underlying soft tissue or skeletal injuries were identified. All the body organs were present in normal anatomical position. The subcutaneous fat layer of the abdominal wall was upto 1/2" thick. There was no internal evidence of blunt force or penetrating injury to the thoraco-abdominal region.

HEAD:
The scalp was reflected and showed extensive subgaleal hemorrhage involving the right fronto-parietal regions. Injury to the skull and brain were mentioned above. The brain on sectioning did not reveal any non-traumatic lesions. The brain weighed 1587 grams.

NECK:
The soft tissues of the neck, including strap muscles, thyroid gland and large vessels revealed no abnormalities. The hyoid bone and larynx were intact.

CARDIOVASCULAR SYSTEM:

The pericardial surfaces were smooth, glistening and unremarkable; the pericardial sac was free of significant fluid or adhesions. The coronary arteries arose normally, followed the usual distribution and were widely patent without thrombus or evidence of atherosclerosis. The chambers and valves exhibit the usual size - position and relationship and were unremarkable. The myocardium was dark red/brown, firm and free of lesions; the atrial and ventricular septae were intact. The aorta and its major branches arose normally followed the usual course and were widely patent, free of significant atherosclerosis or abnormality. The vena cava and its major tributories return to the heart in the usual distribution and are free of thrombi. The heart weighed 338 grams.

RESPIRATORY SYSTEM:

The upper airway was clear of debris and foreign material; the mucosal surfaces were congested. The pleural surfaces were smooth, glistening and the pulmonary parenchyma was markedly congested and edematous. No focal lesions were noted other than in the upper and middle lobes that showed evidence of aspiration of blood. The pulmonary arteries were normally developed, patent without thrombus or embolus. The right lung weighed 1023 grams and the left 619 grams.

LIVER AND BILIARY SYSTEM:

The hepatic capsule was smooth, glistening and intact, covering a red/brown, moderately congested parenchyma which on sectioning did not reveal any focal lesions. The gall bladder contained 10 ml of green mucoid bile; the mucosa was velvety and unremarkable. The extra hepatic biliary tree was patent, without evidence of calculi. The liver weighed 1859 grams.

ALIMENTARY TRACK:

The tongue was without evident recent injury. The esophagus was lined by gray/white, smooth mucosa. The gastric mucosa was arranged in the usual rugal folds and lumen contained 200 ml of light pinkish liquid with pieces of meat. The small and large bowels were unremarkable. The pancreas had a normal tan/pink lobulated appearance and the ducts were patent. The appendix was present and unremarkable.

GENITOURINARY SYSTEM:

The renal capsules were smooth and thin, semi-transparent and stripped with ease from the underlying smooth red/brown, cortical surfaces. The left kidney in its intraparenchymal region (involving the medullary and the cortical regions) had a clear thin walled fluid filled cysts that had a 2 cm diameter. The right kidney did not show any lesions. The cortices were congested but well delineated. The calyces, pelves and ureters were free of lesions. The urinary bladder contained 10 ml of clear yellow urine; the mucosa was tan/gray and wrinkled. The testes, prostate and seminal vesicles were free of lesions and injury. The right kidney weighed 166 grams and the left 219 grams.

RETICULOENDOTHELIAL SYSTEM:

The spleen had a smooth, intact capsule covering a purple, moderately firm parenchyma; the lymphoid follicles were undiscernible. The regional lymph nodes appeared normal. The spleen weighed 171 grams.

ENDOCRINE SYSTEM:

The pituitary, thyroid and adrenal glands were free of lesions.

MUSCULOSKELETAL SYSTEM:

Muscle development was normal. No obvious bone or joint abnormalities were noted other than traumatic injury to the scalp.

MICROSCOPIC EXAMINATION:

Specimens submitted; brain, heart, lung, liver and kidney.

TOXICOLOGIC ANALYSIS:

Specimens submitted; blood, urine, bile, vitreous, stomach contents, liver, brain, spleen and kidney and hospital admission blood. Analysis requested; routine screen.

X-RAYS/PHOTOGRAPHY:

Appropriate photo's were taken of injuries and body. X-rays retain from hospital.

PATHOLOGIC DIAGNOSIS:

A. **Gunshot wound to head.**
    1. Entrance: medial aspect of right upper eyelid.
    2. Injury: skin underlying soft tissue right eye, skull, brain.
    3. Termination: right squamosal part of the temporal bone.
    4. Recovery: deformed large caliber gray metal bullet weight 9.6 grams.
    5. Trajectory: front to back, towards the right and slightly upwards.

B. **Other Injury:**
    Contusion left malar region.

CAUSE OF DEATH:
    Gunshot wound to head.

MANNER OF DEATH:
    Homicide.

Junaid R. Shaikh M.D.,
Associate Medical Examiner

JRS:lsw
DIST: Essex County Prosecutor's Office File (1); JRS (1);
DATE DICTATED: November 10, 1996
DATE TRANSCRIBED: November 14, 1996
DATE FINALIZED: May   06, 1997

07962301.MIC
YAFEU, Fula

MICROSCOPIC REPORT: May 06, 1997

ORGAN	SLIDE #	FINDINGS
Heart	4	No pathologic diagnosis.
Lungs	2	Intraalveolar hemorrhage.
Liver	1	Sinusoidal congestion.
Kidney	3	Congestion.
Brain	5, 6	Fresh contusion, hemorrhage.

Junaid R. Shaikh M.D.,
Associate Medical Examiner

JRS:lsw
DIST: Essex County Prosecutor's Office File (1); JRS (1);

THIS PAGE INTENTIONALLY LEFT BLANK

VOLUNTARY STATEMENT OF LAVIE JOHNSON

Date: November 11, 1996
5 pages
Redactions, asterisks, and underlines within statement are from providing agency.

Yaki was shot in the hallway outside of the apartment where Lavie Johnson lived.

She called Yaasmyn on November 10 to tell her Yaki had been shot in the head. During that phone call to Yaasmyn, she said the last thing she heard Yaki say outside in the hallway was, "Get that gun out my face."

Rashad called her before Yaki came to her home that night and told her to not tell Yaki he was coming by. In spite of this, she did tell Yaki before Rashad arrived.

After Yaki was shot, Rashad called and asked her where did she live because he did not know where she lived. Lavie answered, "You know where I live because you just left here."

Lavie says Rashad and Kaseem arrived in an Irvington Cab because she was told by neighbors that they saw two guys get out of the Irvington Cab and when they left the building, they ran to the corner and got back into the Irvington Cab. This contradicts the statement of Moinville Ovil of the Irvington Cab that he just dropped the two off and did not wait.

Lavie states she knew Yaki wore a bulletproof vest because he said people think he is bad because he raps with Tupac.

Lavie called Rashad's house looking for him and spoke to his brother Sharif Clark. Sharif states Rashad said he didn't kill Yaki, he didn't mean it, it was an accident. He said Kaseem had grabbed Yaki in a choke hold and that Yaki said, "You niggas can't phase me," then Rashad pulled out a gun and shot him.

Lavie states one of Yaki's friends called after the incident and said that he did not think it was a mistake because Rashad was arguing with Yaki in Montclair and said he was going to kill him.

ORANGE POLICE DEPARTMENT
STATEMENT

DATE:11/11/96   TIME:10:20AM   COMPLAINT #:96-29039

VOLUNTARY STATEMENT:LAVIE JOHNSON   AGE:19

RESIDING AT: ███████████████████████████████████████

STATEMENT TAKEN BY:DET JEROME ANDERSON   WITNESSED BY:DET/SGT SODY

Q. WHAT IS YOUR FULL NAME AND DATE OF BIRTH?
A. LAVIE JOHNSON. 052477

Q. WHERE DO YOU RESIDE AND WITH WHOM?
A. ███████████████████████████, MY MOTHER CLAUDIA JOHNSON, MY DAUGHTER
   YUKIYAH JOHNSON (AGE TWO), MY SISTER COLEEN JOHNSON, MY BROTHER
   COLEAF JOHNSON AND MY OTHER BROTHER SELENE JOHNSON.

Q. ARE YOU EMPLOYED? IF SO BY WHOM?
A. NO.

Q. WHAT IS THE HIGHEST LEVEL OF EDUCATION YOU HAVE COMPLETED?
A. 11TH GRADE.

Q. WHAT IS YOUR SOCIAL SECURITY NUMBER?
A. ████████

Q. CAN YOU READ, WRITE AND UNDERSTAND THE ENGLISH LANGUAGE?
A. YES.

Q. MS. LAVIE JOHNSON I AM DETECTIVE ANDERSON OF THE ORANGE POLICE
   DEPARTMENT. I AM GOING TO ASK YOU CERTAIN QUESTION CONCERNING THE
   SHOOTING DEATH OF YAFEU FULA THAT OCCURRED AT ███████████████████
   FLOOR HALLWAY ON 11/10/96. WOULD YOU ANSWER ANY QUESTION REGARDING
   SAME?
A. YES.

Q. WHO IS YAFEU FULA?
A. HE IS MY BOYFRIEND.

Q. WHEN WAS THE LAST TIME YOU SAW YAFEU FULA?
A. AFTER HE GOT SHOT IN THE HALLWAY.

Q. WERE YOU PRESENT WHEN THE SHOOTING TOOK PLACE?
A. I WAS IN MY APARTMENT IN THE BACK ROOM.

Q. HOW DID YOU FIND OUT THAT YAFEU FULA GOT SHOT?
A. AFTER I HEARD A POP NOISE MY MOTHER WENT TO THE DOOR AND SHE CALLED
   ME.

Q. WHAT DID YOU OBSERVE WHEN YOUR MOTHER CALLED YOU TO THE DOOR?
A. I SAW YAFEU LAYING ON HIS BACK IN THE HALL AND WHEN I WALKED TOWARDS

HIM I SAW BLOOD ON HIS FACE.

Q. WHY WAS YAFEU IN THE HALLWAY?
A. YAFEU COUSIN AND A FRIEND CAME OVER.

Q. WHAT TIME DID THEY COME OVER?
A. ABOUT 3:30AM.

Q. DO YOU KNOW THE NAMES OF THE PERSON WHO YOU STATED CAME OVER TO SEE YAFEU?
A. RODDY AND KAS.

Q. DO YOU KNOW THEM BY ANY OTHER NAMES?
A. AFTER YAFEU WAS SHOT I FOUND OUT RODDY NAME WAS RASHAD CLARK.

Q. DID YOU OBSERVE THE TWO GUYS WHO CAME OVER TO SEE YAFEU AT 3:30AM ON 11/10/96?
A. I DIDN'T SEE THEM.

Q. HOW DO YOU KNOW THAT IT WAS THEM WHOM CAME OVER?
A. BECAUSE RODDY CALLED BEFORE YAFEU WAS THERE AND HE SAID DONT TELL YAFEU. AND WHILE YAFEU WAS IN THE HALLWAY WITH THEM RODDY DIDN'T CALL. THEN AFTER YAFEU WAS SHOT RODDY CALLED AND SAID LAVIE WHERE DO YOU LIVE AT I DONT KNOW WHERE YOU LIVE AT. I SAID YOU KNOW WHERE I LIVE AT BECAUSE YOU BEEN TO MY HOUSE BEFORE AND YOU JUST LEFT HERE. HE SAID KNOW I DIDN'T ME AND KAS WAS RIDING AROUND IN A CAB LOOKING FOR YOUR HOUSE. I JUST SLAMMED THE PHONE DOWN BECAUSE I WAS ABOUT TO GO TO THE HOSPITAL.

Q. DID YOU TELL YAFEU THAT RODDY WAS COMING OVER?
A. YES.

Q. WHAT DID YAFEU SAY OR DO WHEN YOU TOLD HIM?
A. HE STARTED LAUGHING AND SAID WORD.

Q. HOW MANY TIMES DID RODDY CALL BEFORE YOU WENT TO THE HOSPITAL?
A. HE CALLED TWICE, ONCE BEFORE YAFEU GOT TO MY APARTMENT AND ONCE AFTER YAFEU WAS SHOT.

Q. WHAT TIME DID RODDY CALL THE FIRST TIME?
A. HE CALLED SOMTIME AFTER 12MIDNIGHT.

Q. WHO SPOKE TO HIM WHEN HE CALLED THE FIRST TIME?
A. KIESHA PERKINS AND TAALIBAH SPENCE.

Q. WHO IS KEISHA PERKINS?
A. SHE IS A FRIEND WHO LIVE SOMEWHERE IN MONTCLAIR.

Q. WHO IS TAALIBAH SPENCE?
A. MY FRIEND.

Q. WHERE DO SHE LIVE?
A. 183 NEW STREET ORANGE.

Q. WHAT TIME DID YAFEU ARRIVE AT YOUR APARTMENT?
A. ABOUT TEN OR FIFTEEN MINUTES BEFORE RODDY AND KAS CAME.

Q. SO WHAT TIME WOULD THAT BE?
A. LITTLE AFTER 3:00AM.

Q. WERE KIESHA AND TAALIBAH PRESENT AT YOUR APARTMENT AT THE TIME YOU
   SAW YAFEU ON THE HALLWAY FLOOR?
A. KIESHA HAD LEFT BEFORE YAFEU CAME IN THE HOUSE. TAALIBAH WAS IN THE
   HOUSE.

Q. HOW LONG HAVE YOU KNOWN RODDY?
A. FOR ABOUT A MONTH OR TWO.

Q. DESCRIBE RODDY?
A. HE IS SHORT, BROWN SKINNED, HE IS THIN, I THINK HE HAS A BALD HEAD,
   AND HE TOLD ME BEFORE THAT HE WAS SISTEEN.

Q. DID YOU FIND OUT SOMETIME LATER THAT THE PERSON WHO YOU KNOW AS RODDY
   IS ALSO KNOWN AS RASHAD CLARK?
A. YES.

Q. WHEN DID YOU FIND THIS OUT?
A. KIESHA TOLD ME BECAUSE KIESHA KNEW RODDY FROM MONTCLAIR.

Q. CAN YOU DESCRIBE KAS TO ME?
A. KNOW I NEVER MET KAS BEFORE.

Q. DID YOU SEE THE TWO GUYS WHO CAME TO YOUR MOTHER'S APARTMENT THE
   MORNING YAFEU GOT SHOT?
A. KNOW, I JUST HEARD THEIR VOICES AT THE DOOR.

Q. DID YOU RECOGNIZE THE VOICES?
A. YES.

Q. WHICH VOICE DID YOU RECOGNIZE?
A. I RECOGNIZED RODDY'S VOICE

Q. WHERE WERE YOU WHEN THEY FIRST CAME TO YOUR DOOR?
A. I WAS IN THE BACK ROOM WHEN I HEARD THE KNOCKING AT THE DOOR.
   I THEN LISTEN TO SEE IF I COULD HEAR WHO WAS AT THE DOOR BECAUSE I
   KNEW RODDY WAS COMING OVER AND I WANTED TO KNOW IF IT WAS HIM BECAUSE
   IT WAS LATE.

Q. WHAT IS THE RELATIONSHIP BETWEEN YAFEU AND RODDY?
A. BEFORE YAFEU WAS KILLED I HEARD HE WAS HIS COUSIN. BUT SINCE YAFEU
   WAS KILLED I FOUND OUT HE WAS YAFEU COUSIN COUSIN.

Q. DO YOU KNOW OF ANYONE WHO MIGHT WANT TO HARM YAFEU?
A. A LOT OF PEOPLE WHO KNOW HIM DIDN'T LIKE HIM BECAUSE HE RAPPED.

Q. WHAT DO YOU MEAN WHEN YOU SAY RAP?
A. MUSIC.

Q. DO YOU KNOW HOW THEY GOT TO YOUR APARTMENT?
A. IN A IRVINGTON CAB.

Q. HOW DO YOU KNOW THEY CAME IN A IRVINGTON CAB

A. BECAUSE DERRICK AND ALEX TOLD ME THEY SAW TWO GUYS GET OUT OF THE IRVINGTON CAB AND WHEN THEY LEFT THE BUILDING THEY RAN AROUND THE CORNER AND GOT BACK INTO THE IRVINGTON CAB.

Q. DO YOU KNOW WHY YAFEU WAS WEARING A BULLET PROOF VEST?
A. BECAUSE HE SAID PEOPLE SAID THAT HE THINK HE IS BAD BECAUSE HE RAPS WITH TUPAC.

Q. DO YOU KNOW IF YAFEU WAS INVOLVED WITH DRUGS?
A. AS FAR AS I KNOW HE IS NOT INVOLVED WITH DRUGS.

Q. SINCE THE SHOOTING HAVE YOU RECEIVED ANY FURTHER INFORMATION

REGARDING WHAT HAPPENED?
A. I CALLED RODDY HOUSE LOOKING FOR RODDY BUT HIS BROTHER SHARIFF ANSWER THE PHONE AND I ASKED FOR RODDY. SHARIFF ASKED WHY YOU WANT TO TALK TO RODDY AND I SAID BECAUSE RODDY KILLED YAFEU. HE THEN PUT THE PHONE AWAY FROM HIS MOUTH AS IF HE WAS TALKING TO RODDY. THEN HE SAID THAT RODDY SAID HE DIDN'T KILL YAFEU, HE DIDN'T MEAN IT. IT WAS AN ACCIDENT. HE SAID THAT THE BOY KAS HAD GRABBED YAFEU IN A CHOKE HOLD AND HE SAID THAT YAFEU SAID YOU NIGGAS CANT PHASE ME. THEN SHARIFF SAID RODDY PULLED OUT A GUN AND MADE A MISTAKE AND SHOT HIM.

Q. DID YOU EVER TALK TO RODDY SINCE THE SECOND TIME HE CALLED YOUR HOUSE AFTER YAFEU WAS SHOT?
A. NO.

Q. MS. JOHNSON I AM NOW SHOWING YOU A PHOTO ARRAY MARKED NUMBER A, IF YOU RECOGNIZE ANYONE IN THE PHOTO WOULD YOU PLEASE INDICATE SAME?
A. I DONT RECOGNIZE ANYONE.

Q. MS. JOHNSON I AM NOW SHOWING YOU ANOTHER PHOTO ARRAY MARKED B, IF YOU RECOGNIZE ANYONE AMONG THESE PHOTOGHRAPS WOULD YOU PLEASE INDICATE SAME?
A. NUMBER 4 IS RODDY.

Q. WHY DO YOU RECOGNIZE THIS PERSON WHO YOU JUST IDENTIFIED?
A. BECAUSE HE IS RODDY, AND I ALSO KNOW HIM AS RASHAD CLARK.

Q. DO YOU KNOW WHERE HE LIVE?
A. YES, 23 NADEN AVENUE IRVINGTON.

Q. MS LAVIE JOHNSON ARE YOU AWARE OF ANY THREATS THAT WERE MADE AGAINST YAFEU FULA?
A. ONE OF YAFEU FRIENDS CALLED ME AFTER HE WAS KILLED AND SAID THAT HE DONT THINK IT WAS A MISTAKE BECAUSE RODDY WAS ARGUING WITH YAFEU IN MONTCLAIR AND SAID HE WAS GOING TO KILL HIM.

Q. WHO IS THE PERSON WHO TOLD YOU THIS ABOUT RODDY?
A. GARFIELD, AND HE LIVE SOMEWHERE IN MONTCLAIR.

Q. HOW DO YOU KNOW ABOUT THIS THREAT?
A. FROM A FRIEND OF MINE AND YAFEU.

Q. WHERE DID THIS THREAT TAKE PLACE?
A. GARF TOLD ME IT HAPPENED AT THE EXON STATION IN MONTCLAIR.

Q. MS LAVIE JOHNSON DO YOU WISH TO ADD ANYTHING FURTHER TO THIS
STATEMENT AT THIS TIME?

A. NO.

Q. DID YOU GIVE THIS STATEMENT OF YOUR OWN FREE WILL?

A. YES.

Q. WERE THERE ANY THREATS OR PROMISES MADE TO YOU DURING THE GIVEN OF
THIS STATEMENT?

A. NO.

Q. IS THIS STATEMENT THE TRUTH TO THE BEST OF YOUR KNOWLEDGE?

A. YES.

Q. ARE YOU WILLING TO TESTIFY IN THE COURT OF LAW REGARDING CONTENTS OF
THIS STATEMENT?

A. YES.

Q. AFTER READING, MAKING CORRECTIONS WHERE IS NEEDED AND CONFIRMING THE
ACCURACY OF THIS STATEMENT. WILL YOU NOW SIGN SAME?

A. YES.

LAVIE JOHNSON   DET. JEROME ANDERSON   DET/SGT. KEVIN SOOY

STATEMENT ENDED
1350HRS

VOLUNTARY STATEMENT OF CLAUDIA LOREN JOHNSON, PART I

Date: November 11, 1996
3 pages
Redactions within statement are from publisher. Asterisks and underlines are from providing agency.
Spelling corrections noted and initialed by Claudia Johnson.

Claudia Johnson is Lavie Johnson's mother. It was her home where the shooting took place.

Yaki had just come to her home, did not have time to take off his coat, and had gone right back out into the hall when she heard the gunshot.

The neighbor said he witnessed the two guys get out of a Irvington Cab and when they left, they got back into the same cab around the corner. This contradicts the statement of Moinville Ovil, the cab driver who dropped off Rashad and Kaseem.

Her statement says that after the shooting, Rashad called her house and she hung up the phone. He called right back and asked for Lavie. She told him Lavie was not there and asked him wasn't he just at her house. Rashad said no. She responded yes you were. Rashad hung up the phone.

She states her daughter Lavie told her Rashad called before he came over and told her to tell Yaki he was coming over and not to tell him.

She states "guy downstairs said they got out of an Irvington Cab and got back in the same cab."

After shooting, she confirms Rashad kept calling back, denying to Claudia he was just there.

DATE: 11/11/96   TIME: 1017 hours   COMPLAINT # 96-29039   PAGE 1 OF

VOLUNTARY STATEMENT: Claudia Loren Johnson   AGE: 38 yrs. old

RESIDING AT: 325 Mechenic Street, Apt. 310, Orange   PHONE # 673█

STATEMENT TAKEN BY: Inv. Howard Johnson   WITNESSED BY: Det. Mosby

I am Investigator Howard Johnson of the Essex County Prosecutor's Office. I would like to ask you some questions regarding a shooting incident, which occurred at 325 Mechenic Street, in Orange, on November 10, 1996.

Q. Would you answer my questions?
A. Yes.

Q. What is your date of birth, and your social security number?
A. January 7, 1959. ████████

Q. Can you read, write, and understand the English language?
A. Yes.

Q. How long have you resided at your current address?
A. Ummm, seven years.

Q. Who lives with you at your present address?
A. Ah, Lavie Johnson, my daughter, my granddaughter, Yukiyah Johnson, ah, Colleen Johnson, My daughter, Coleaf Johnson, my son, Selene Johnson, my son. My daughter's girlfriend Taalibah Spence stays with us sometimes.

Q. Where does Taalibah Spence live?
A. 183 New Street, in Orange.

Q. What was the last school which you attended?
A. Essex County College.

Q. What is the highest grade level that you have completed?
A. I finished two years of college.

Q. Were you present during a shooting, which occurred in 325 Mechenic Street, on the third floor on 11/10/96?
A. Yes.

Q. Do you know the person's name who was shot?
A. Yeah, Yafeu Fula.

Q. What was your relationship to the victim?
A. Um, a friend, he dated my daughter Lavie.

Q. Can you tell me what he was doing prior to the shooting?
A. He had just came in the door, and he was talking to Lavie, and Taalibah in the bedroom.

Q. Would you tell me what happened leading to the shooting?
A. Umm, there was a knock on the door, and Yafeu went to the door, and I followed behind him. He answered the door, and he said, "what's up to his friends". I told Yafeu to tell his friends r to make so much noise, because it was too late. Yaf told them to be quite, as he was telling them to be quite, the puppy was on his way out of the door, and one of the two boys reached

A. (continued) down and touched the puppy, and the puppy bit him. When the bit him, the boy sa
oh you got a fake pitbull, and Yaf picked the dog up.

Q. Can you describe the two boys who came to your door?
A. Umm Huh, ahh the short one, he was dark skinned, he had a hat on, either dark blue, or black,
he had on a dark jacket, and he didn't have on glasses, but if I saw his face, I would remembe

Q. Would you describe the second boy to me?
A. He was maybe my height, 5'04", he was thin, umm, he was light skinned, he had a hat on, it
looked liked he had a bald head, umm, he had on a green jacket, and he looked liked like he wa
maybe seventeen years old.

Q. Had you ever seen either of the two boys prior to then?
A. No.

Q. Had either of these two boys telephoned your house prior to that visit?
A. I didn't talk to them, but Lavie, and Taalibah said that they did.

Q. Do you know if Lavie, or Taalibah know either of the boys?
A. Umm, I'm not shure, but I think the little short one, because when I told them who was at the
door, I told Lavie that he reminded me of someone named Irammin, and she said that it must hav
been Roddy. She found out that his real name is Rashan Clark.

Q. Would you continue from the point that the boy picked up the puppy?
A. Umm, Yaf picked up the puppy, and I turned and went back into the room with Lavie. That's whe
I told Lavie about the guy that looked like Irammin, but I know that he wasn't. I was walking
to my room, and I heard the gunshot. Umm, It was low, it sounded like something fell, like a
bottle, and I went to the door, and I saw Yaf Lying on the floor. I told Lavie to come and ch
Yaf, he was shot. I went, and call 911, and that's it. He didn't even have time to take off
coat, he just came in, and went right back out into the hall. The guy downstairs said that
they got out of a Irvington cab, they also said that the cab was around the corner, and they
got back into the same cab.

Q. Would you be able to recognize both, or either of the two boys who came to your house?
A. Umm, I think so.

Q. Can you tell me the time which the incident occurred?
A. Umm, I think it was between 0315, and 0330 in the morning?

Q. Did you ever see, or speak to either of the two boys after the shooting?
A. I spoke Roddy twice. The first time, Lavie was at the hospital, and he said," Lavie, why you
keep hanging up the phone on me", and I told him that this was not Lavie, this is her mother,
and I hung the phone up. He called right back, and he asked for Lavie, and I told him that
Lavie wasn't here, and I asked him wasn't you just at my house, and he said no. I told him
yes you were, cause I seen you, and he hung the phone up. that was it.

Q. Do you have a caller I.D. unit, which would document the telephone calls?
A. Yes, I have the deluxe, it gives the person's name, and the telephone number.

Q. Did you give members of the Orange Police Department permission to take the unit?

A. (continued) Yes.

Q. Would you tell me who was present in your appartment during the shooting incident?
A. Umm, Lavie, Colleen, Taalibah, Yukiyah, Danielle, my cousin, and Kiesha was there before Yaf got there, but she left.

Q. Do you know anyone who would want to hurt Yafeu?
A. No I don't.

Q. What is the man's name who told you about the cab from Irvington?
A. Umm, I know him as Skipper, I don't know his first name.

Q. Has anyone contacted you regarding the shooting with information?
A. Umm, Roddy's cousin called, and I told him that I think that it was his cousin that shot Ya

Q. Who's cousin shot Yaf?
A. I told Mutah that I think that his cousin Roddy shot Yaf.

Q. Who is Mutah, and what is his entire name, and address?
A. I don't know his whole name, but he called me from Atlanta. Mutahis Yaf's cousin, andMutah is also Roddy's cousin. Mutah gave me his cousin's name, address, telephone number, and sa told call Roddy's grandfather, and tell him that I was going to call the police, and that I going to identify him.

Q. Would you give me the information, that Mutah told you?
A. He said that Roddy's real name is Rashad Clark, he lives at 23 Naden Avenue, in Irvington, his telephone number is 375-2341.

Q. How often would Yafeu come to your house?
A. About five days out of the week.

Q. Q. Is there anything that you wish to add to your statement?
A. Lavie told me that Roddy called before he came over, and he told her to tell Yaf, that he w coming over, then he said not to tell him.

Q. Have any threats, or promises been made to you for you to give this statement?
A. No.

Q. Do you affirm that the information which you have just provided, is the whole truth, and yc do so under penalty of the law?
A. Yes.

Q. At the conclusion of this statement, would you read, make corrections, and when you are completely satisfied that it contains exactly what you have told me, would you sign your statement?
A. Yes.
Statement enden at 1219 hours, on 11/11/96.

Date: November 11, 1996
1 page
Handwritten correction by Claudia Johnson as provided by Orange Police Department.

She identifies Kaseem in a photo lineup as a person who came to her house around 3:15 or 3:30am.

ORANGE POLICE DEPARTMENT

Statement

DATE: 11/11/96 _____ TIME: 1251 hours ___ COMPLAINT #96-29039 ___ PAGE 1 OF ____

VOLUNTARY STATEMENT: Claudia Loren Johnson _____ AGE: 38 ____

RESIDING AT: 325 Mechenic Street, apt. 310, Orange ___ PHONE # _____

STATEMENT TAKEN BY: Inv. Howard Johnson _____ WITNESSED BY: Det. Mosby ____

). Ms. Johnson we spoke earlier about two boys that came to your apartment door, to see Yafeu Fula would you be able to recognize those boys if you saw photographs of them?
.. I may be, I'm not sure.

'. I am now showing you photo array marked #A, of six black males, numbered 1-6, and if you recognize anyone, would you let me know?
. Yes.

). Do you recognize anyone?
.. Yes number three , and number four, but I'd pick number three, because hi face is fuller.

'. What do you remember number three doing, or where do you know hem from?
.. I don't know him, he was at the doorthe night that Yaf got shot.

'. Would you sign, and date the rear of photo number three, indicating that you have identified the person as being the person that you saw the night of the shooting?
. Yes. (Ms. Johnson complies, and signs, and dates the rear of photo number three(Kasseem Nadir). then initials the remaining five photos.

. I am now showing you a second photo arry of another six black males, and if you recognize anyone in this array would you let me know?
I don't recognize anyone. (Ms. Johnson doesn't recognize anyone in array B).

Is there anything that you wish to add to your statement?
No.

Do you affirm that the information which you have just provided is the whole truth, and you do under penalty of the law?
Yes.

Have any threats or promises been made to you for you to give this statement?
No.

At the conclusion of your statement would you read, make any corrections, and when your satisfie that the information is exactly what you have told me, would you sign your statement?
Yes.
tement concluded at 1347 hours on 11/11/96...

ESSEX CO. PROSECUTOR'S OFFICE
PRELIMINARY REPORT

Dated: November 12, 1996
1 page

Yaki was transported to University Hospital where he succumbed to his injuries.

No arrests made as of the date of the report.

Investigation is open.

ESSEX COUNTY PROSECUTOR'S OFFICE
HOMICIDE SECTION

PRELIMINARY REPORT

INVESTIGATOR	DATE	SECTION #
HOWARD JOHNSON	11/12/96	H#122-96

[XX] Homicide   [ ] Special Investigation

DECEASED/SUBJECT

CC# 96-29039

NAME: YAFEU A. FULA
AGE: 19YRS OLD   RACE: BLACK/MALE

HOUR OF INCIDENT: 0348
DAY OF WEEK: SUNDAY
DATE: MONTH: 11   DAY: 10   YEAR: 96

LOCATION: 325 MECHANIC STREET, 3RD FLOOR, ORANGE
TYPE OF INCIDENT: SHOOTING DEATH

SYNOPSIS:

ON November 10, 1996, Yafeu A. Fula, was the victim of a
single gunshot wound to the head.

Apparently the victim, and two young men were in the hallway
of 325 Mechanic Street, near apartment 310, when a single gunshot
was heard by witnesses.

The victim was transported to University Hospital were he
succumbed to his injuries.

The victim was pronounced dead at 1300 hours on November 10
1996, by Dr. Oruwari. This investigation is open and pending
further investigation.

ARREST MADE: NONE AT THIS TIME.

Respectfully submitted,

_____   _____
Supervisor's Approval   HOWARD JOHNSON
                                  COUNTY INVESTIGATOR
HJ:dvk

VOLUNTARY STATEMENT OF ROBERT SKIPPER

Date: November 12, 1996
3 pages
Redactions within statement made by publisher to protect personal information. Handwritten corrections by Robert Skipper.

Robert Antwan Skipper resided in the building on Mechanic Street.

He heard one shot and went into the hallway to see Yaki laying on the ground.. He identified Kaseem in a photo lineup.

He observed Kaseem and another person go into the building on 11/10/96. After he heard the gunshot, he saw them both run out of the building and around the corner.

ORANGE POLICE DEPARTMENT

Statement

DATE: 11-12-96   TIME: 11:10 A.M. COMPLAINT # 96-29039   PAGE 1 OF 3

VOLUNTARY STATEMENT: ROBERT ANTWAN SKIPPER   AGE: 21

RESIDING AT: 339 MECHANIC STREET APT.404 ORANGE N. PHONE # 677-▮▮▮

STATEMENT TAKEN BY: SGT.SOOY   WITNESSED BY: DET.MOSBY

Q. WHAT IS YOUR FULL NAME AND DATE OF BIRTH?
A. ROBERT ANTWAN SKIPPER 09-25-75.

Q. WHERE DO YOU LIVE AND WITH WHOM?
A. I LIVE AT 339 MECHANIC STREET APT.404 WITH MY SISTER SHANDA SKIPPER.

Q. ARE YOU EMPLOYED AND IF SO BY WHOM?
A. NO I ATTEND SCHOOL.

Q. HOW FAR HAVE YOU GONE IN SCHOOL?
A. 2nd YEAR OF COLLEGE AT PHIFIER UNIVERSITY NORTH CAROLINA.

Q. CAN YOU READ, WRITE AND UNDERSTAND THE ENGLISH LANGUAGE?
A. YES

Q. MR. SKIPPER ON SUNDAY 11-10-96 AT APPROXIMATELY 03:48 A.M. A SHOOTING OCCURED AT 325 MECHANIC STREET IS THIS CORRECT?
A. YES.

Q. IN YOUR OWN WORDS CAN YOU TELL ME WHAT YOU WITNESSED CONCERNING THIS SHOOTING?
A. I HAD JUST COME HOME FROM THE MOVIES, I PARKED MY SISTERS CAR IN THE PARKING LOT AND WAS WALKING TOWARDS THE BUILDING, WHEN I GOT NEAR THE DOORS AT THE 339 SIDE OF THE BUILDING I NOTICED AN IRVINGTON CAB PULLED UP AND TWO GUYS GOT OUT OF IT AND WALKED INTO THE 325 SIDE OF THE BUILDING. AS I GOT UP TO MY FLOOR I WAS JUST ABOUT TO OPEN MY APARTMENT DOOR WHEN I HEARD A GUN SHOT GO OFF. AFTER I HEARD THIS SHOT I RAN BACK DOWNSTAIRS AND THATS WHEN I SAW THE SAME TWO GUYS RUNNING OUT OF THE BUILDING. AFTER THEY RAN OUT OF THE BUILDING THEY RAN AROUND THE CORNER TO ESSEX AVENUE TOWARD THE HOSPITAL. AS I WAS STANDING IN FRONT OF THE BUILDING THESE TWO GIRLS WERE HOLLERING OUT OF THEIR BATHROOM WINDOW "DID YOU SEE ANYBODY RUN OUT OF THE BUILDING" AT FIRST I THOUGHT THEY WERE ONLY KIDDING, THEN SHE ASKED ME AGAIN AND I TOLD THEM THAT I SAW SOMEBODY RUNNING OUT OF THE BUILDING. THEN I WENT INTO THE BUILDING ON THE 325 SIDE TO SEE WHAT HAPPENED AND AS I WAS GOING UP STAIRS I SAW THE BODY LAYING IN THE THIRD FLOOR HALLWAY RIGHT NEAR THE ELEVATOR. I SAW A HOLE IN THE FRONT OF HIS HEAD NEAR HIS EYE AND RAN BACK DOWN STAIRS BECAUSE I WAS SCARED. WHEN I GOT BACK DOWNSTAIRS I SAW THE POLICE AND TOLD THEM WHAT SIDE TO GO IN AND TO GO TO THE THIRD FLOOR. AFTER THAT I WENT BACK UPSTAIRS TO SEE WHAT WAS GOING ON AND JUST HUNG OUT FOR A WHILE.

Q. CAN YOU TELL ME HOW MANY GUN SHOTS YOU HEARD?
A. ONE

Q. DID YOU SEE ANYONE WITH A GUN EITHER BEFORE OR AFTER THE SHOOTING?
A. NO

ROBERT ANTWAN SKIPPER _Robert Skipper_   SGT.K.SOOY _[signature]_

DET.T.MOSBY _[signature]_

Q. DO YOU REALISE THIS IS PAGE TWO OF YOUR STATEMENT?
A. YES

Q. CAN YOU DESCRIBE THE CAB YOU SAW THE TWO PERSON GET OUT OF?
A. IT WAS YELLOW COLOR AND HAD IRVINGTON CAB ON THE SIDE.

Q. DID YOU SEE WHERE THE CAB WENT AFTER IT DROPPED THESE TWO PERSONS OFF?
A. IT WENT STRAIGHT DOWN MECHANIC STREET TOWARD LINCOLN AVENUE AND MADE A LEFT ONTO LINCOLN AVENUE.

Q. CAN YOU DESCRIBE THE TWO PERSONS WHO GOT OUT OF THE CAB?
A. THEY WERE BOTH BLACL MALES, THE DARK SKINNED ONE WAS ABOUT 5'9" TALL, HE WAS WEARING A GREEN AND BROWN COLOR ARMY JACKET, A BLACK WOOL SKULLY HAT, BLACK JEANS HE LOOKED LIKE HE WAS BETWEEN 18-20 YEARS OLD.
THE LIGHT SKINNED ONE WAS WEARING A BLUE AND BLACK NORT FACE JACKET, A BLACK SKULLY WOOL HAT AND I THINK HE WAS WEARING BLUE JEANS, HE WAS ABOUT THE SAME HEIGHT AS THE OTHER GUY.

Q. IS THIS THE FIRST TIME YOU EVER SAW EITHER OF THE PERSONS YOU DESCRIBED?
A. YES.

Q. I AM NOW GOING TO SHOW YOU TWO SIX WAY PHOTO FOLDER ARRAYS, AFTER LOOKING AT THESE PHOTOS CAN YOU IDENTIFY ANY OF THE PERSONS AS THE ONES WHO YOU PREVIOUS DESCRIBED?
A. YES THE LIGHT SKINNED ONE LOOKS LIKE THE PERSON IN PHOTO #3

Q. CAN YOU TELL ME WHAT PHOTO ARRAY FOLDER YOU FOUND THIS PERSON IN?
A. THE FOLDER MARKED A AND THE PHOTO IS NUMBER 3.
NOTE: PHOTO IDENTIFIED IS NADIR KASSEEM WAY D.O.B. 8-8-79 LKA 479 UNION AVENUE IRVINGTON N.J.

Q. AS PART OF THIS INVESTIGATION I AM GOING TO ASK YOU TO SIGN AND DATE THE BACK OF TH EPHOTO YOU IDENTIFIED, WOULD YOU SIGN AND DATE THE BACK OF THIS PHOTO?
A. YES.

Q. AFTER LOOKING THROUGH THESE PHOTO ARRAYS WERE YOU ABLE TO IDENTIFY THE OTHER PERSON YOU DESCRIBED?
A. NO.   R.S

Q. CAN YOU TELL ME WHO THE TWO GIRLS WERE WHO WERE ASKING YOU IF YOU SAW ANYONE RUN OUT OF THE BUILDING?
A. I DON'T KNOW WHO IT WAS BUT IT WAS SOMEONE IN APARTMENT #310 ON THE 325 SIDE OF MECHANIC STREET.

ROBERT ANTWAN SKIPPER   _Robert Skipper_   SGT.K.SOOY _Sgt. Sooy_

DET.T.MOSBY _Det. T. Mosby_

Q. DO YOU REALISE THIS IS PAGE THREE OF YOUR STATEMENT?
A. YES.

Q. CAN YOU TELL ME EXACTLY WHAT YOU SAW THE PERSON YOU IDNETIFIED IN PHOTO ARRAY LABELED A PHOTO #3 DO ON THE DATE OF THIS INCIDENT?
A. I ONLY SAW HIM GET OUT OF THE CAB WITH THE OTHER GUY I DESCRIBED AND GO INTO THE BUILDING ON THE 325 SIDE AND AFTER I HEARD THE GUN SHOT GO OFF I SAW THEM BOTH RUN OUT OF THE BUILDING ONTO ESSEX AVENUE IN THE DIRECTION OF THE HOSPITAL.

Q. DO YOU KNOW WHY THIS PERSON WAS SHOT?
A. NO

Q. DO YOU KNOW WHO SHOT THIS PERSON?
A. NO

Q. IS THERE ANYTHING ELSE YOU WOULD LIKE TO TELL ME?
A. NO

Q. IS THIS STATEMENT THE TRUTH THE WHOLE TRUTH SO HELP YOU GOD?
A. YES

ROBERT ANTWAN SKIPPER _Robert Skipper_   SGT.K.SOOY _[signature]_

DET.T.MOSBY _[signature]_

VOLUNTARY STATEMENT OF MOINVILLE OVIL

Date: November 13, 1996
3 pages
Redactions within statement made by publisher to protect personal information. Handwritten asterisks are from providing agency.

Moinville Ovil was dispatched from the Irvington Cab Company to pick up a fare at 23 Naden Avenue, the residence of Rashad Clark.

He states upon picking up Rashad he was directed to go to Chancellor and Union Streets in Irvington to pick up a second passenger.

The second passenger was there waiting for him.

This contradicts the 11/14/96 statement of Rashad where he states when he entered the Irvington Cab at his residence and he directed the cab to proceed to the Mechanic Street Projects located in Orange, but then Clark saw Kaseem on the way and called to him and Kaseem entered the cab.

DATE:	TIME:	PLACE:	FILE NO:
11/13/96	0253 hrs.	ESSEX COUNTY PROSECUTOR'S OFFICE	HOM118-96

VOLUNTARY STATEMENT OF:	AGE:
Moinville Ovil	34 yrs. old

RESIDENCE:	PHONE:
23-25 Robert Place, 1ST floor, Irvington	416-8559

OCCUPATION:	EMPLOYER:
Cab Driver	Irvington Cab Company

STATEMENT MADE TO:
Inv. Howard Johnson Essex County Prosecutor's Office

I am Investigator Howard Johnson of the Essex County Prosecutor's Office. I would like to ask you some questions regarding circumstances surrounding a shooting, which occurred at 325 Mechenic Street, in Orange, on November 10, 1996.

Q. Would you answer my questions?
A. Yes.

Q. Can you read, write, and understand the English language?
A. Yes.

Q. How long have you lived at your present address?
A. Four years.

Q. Who do you live with at your present address?
A. I live by myself.

Q. Do you have any relatives in the area?
A. Yeah.

Q. Where does your closet relative live, and what is their name?
A. My brother Silibon Ovil, and he lives at the same address as me.

Q. Where are you originally from?
A. Haiti.

Q. What is your date of birth, and your social security number?
A. My date of birth is 07/01/1962. My social security is █████████

Q. How long have you worked for Irvington Cab Company?
A. Ahh, about eight years now.

Q. On Sunday morning November 10th, at about 2:30 am, did you pick up a fare at 23 Naden Avenue, in Irvington?
A. Yes.

Q. Were you dispatched there, or did you pick the fare up from the street?
A. The dispatcher sent me to the address to get the fare.

Q. Can you describe the person, or persons you picked up at that location?
A. Ahh, the one I picked up at the house, I can't lie to you I really didn't see his face, because he got in the backdoor. Ahh, the first one made me stop to pick up another passenger, and if you show me a picture I can tell you who he is.

Q. Where did the first ask you to go to pick up the second passenger?

SWORN AND SUBSCRIBED TO BEFORE ME THIS

13th DAY OF NOVEMBER 96   _Moinville Ovil_
                                SIGNATURE

THIS AFFIDAVIT TAKEN PURSUANT TO CHAPTER 39 OF THE LAWS OF 1953

OFFICE OF THE ESSEX COUNTY PROSECUTOR

NEWARK, NJ

DATE	TIME	PLACE	FILE NO
11/13/96	0253 hrs.	ESSEX COUNTY PROSECUTOR'S OFFICE	HOM118-96

VOLUNTARY STATEMENT OF	AGE
Moinville Ovil	34 yrs. old

RESIDENCE	PHONE
23-25 Robert Place, 1ST floor, Irvington	416-8559

OCCUPATION	EMPLOYER
Cab Driver	Irvington Cab Company

STATEMENT MADE TO
Inv. Howard Johnson Essex County Prosecutor's Office

A. Umm, Chancellor, and Union.

Q. Was the second passenger there waiting for you, or did you have to wait for him?
A. He was waiting for him.

Q. Where did you take the two men, after the second passenger got into your cab?
A. I don't remember the address, but it was Mechenic Street. It was the Projects.

Q. Do you remember what the fare was?
A. Twelve dollars.

Q. Did either of the two men ask you to wait for them?
A. No.

Q. Do you remember what the two men were talking about?
A. No.

Q. Did the two men seem happy, or serious?
A. They were serious.

Q. Did you see either of the two men with a gun?
A. No.

Q. Did the two men go directly into the building, after they got out of your cab?
A. I don't know. As soon as they got of the cab, I took off man.

Q. Did you think that the two men were going to do something to you?
A. No.

Q. Can you describe what the first passenger was wearing?
A. No.

Q. Can you describe what the second passenger was wearing?
A. Yeah, he was wearing a black jacket, and a black knit cap.

Q. Can you describe the second man?
A. He was skinny, like me, and he was light skinned.

Q. I am now showing you a photo array marked #A of six black males. Would you let me know if you recognize anyone in the array?
A. Yes.

Q. Do you recognize anyone?
A. No.

SWORN AND SUBSCRIBED TO BEFORE ME THIS

13th DAY OF NOVEMBER 19 96   _Moinville Ovil_
                              SIGNATURE

THIS AFFIDAVIT TAKEN PURSUANT TO CHAPTER 39 OF THE LAWS OF 1953

DATE	TIME	PLACE	
11/13/96	0253 hrs.	ESSEX COUNTY PROSECUTOR'S OFFICE	FILE NO. HOM118-96

VOLUNTARY STATEMENT OF	
Moinville Ovil	AGE. 34 yrs. old

RESIDENCE: 23-25 Robert Place, 1ST floor, Irvington   **PHONE:** 416-8559

OCCUPATION: Cab Driver   **EMPLOYER:** Irvington Cab Company

STATEMENT MADE TO: Inv. Howard Johnson Essex County Prosecutor's Office

Q. I am now showing a second array of six black males, marked #B. Would you let me know if you recognize anyone in this array?
A. Yeah.

Q. Do you recognize anyone?
A. No.

Q. Did the man who got into the cab on Naden Avenue, come out of a house?
A. Yes.

Q. Do you remember what house he came out of?
A. 23 Naden.

Q. Are you sure that your fare exited 23 Naden Avenue, in Irvington?
A. Yes, 23.

Q. Was anyone with him when he exited 23 Naden Avenue?
A. Ahh, when I first get there, a young lady said," wait a minute, he's coming right out".

Q. Is there anything else that you wish to add to your statement?
A. Ahh, what I want to say is I just come here. I don't know what happened.

Q. Do you swear, or affirm, that the information which you have just provided is the whole truth, and you do so under penalty of the law?
A. Yes.

Q. Have any threats, or promises been made to you for you to give this statement?
A. No.

Q. At the conclusion of the statement, would you read, make corrections, and when your satisfied that the statement contains exactly what you have told me. Would you sign it?
A. Yeah I will sign it.
Statement ended at 0345 hours on November 13, 1996..

SWORN AND SUBSCRIBED TO BEFORE ME THIS

_13th_ DAY OF _NOVEMBER_ 19_96_   SIGNATURE _Moinville Ovil_

THIS AFFIDAVIT TAKEN PURSUANT TO CHAPTER 39 OF THE LAWS OF 1953

TOXICOLOGY REPORT

Date: November 13, 1996
1 page

Results show nothing detected in blood nor urine.

STATE OF NEW JERSEY
STATE TOXICOLOGY LABORATORY
EDWIN H. ALBANO INSTITUTE OF FORENSIC SCIENCE
325 Norfolk Street
Newark, New Jersey 07103

201-648-3915

TOXICOLOGY REPORT

Lab No: 96-3138   Received: 11-13-96 1132 jas

Name: FULA, Yafeu   COYRSEQNO: 07-96-2301/NA
Age: 19   Sex: M Race: B   Posted by: SHAIKH

Specimens submitted: Blood, urine, bile, vitreous, brain, liver, kidney,
stomach-content, spleen, premortem-blood.

Analysis requested : Alcohols

RESULTS: Report Date: 2:31 PM MON., 18 NOV., 1996

BLOOD:

   Not Detected -
     Volatiles: Acetone,Ethanol,Isopropanol,Methanol.

URINE:

   Not Detected -
     Drugs and other compounds: Amphetamine,Barbiturates,Benzodiazepines,Cannabinoids,Cocaine metabolites,
     Methadone,Methamphetamine,Opiates,Phencyclidine (PCP),Phenytoin,Propoxyphene,TCAntidepressants.

PREMORTEM-BLOOD:

   Not Detected -
     Volatiles: Acetone,Ethanol,Isopropanol,Methanol.

/jr
96-3138

                              Reng-lang Lin, Ph.D.,
                              CHIEF TOXICOLOGIST

ARREST REPORT OF NADIR KASEEM WAY

Date: November 13, 1996
1 page
Redactions by providing agency.

Arrest took place at Essex County Prosecutor's Office.

INCIDENT REPORT

1) POLICE AGENCY

ORANGE P.D.

3) PREV. CC NO.
96-29039

4) VICTIM OR OBJECT OF REPORT
Juvenile Arrest

5) RES. PHONE NO.

6) BUS. PHONE NO.

7) Page 1 of 1

8) ADDRESS OF VICTIM OR OBJECT OF REPORT
City of Orange Police Department

D.O.B.

9) APT. NO.

10) FLOOR

14) SOC.SEC#

15) CRIME OR INCIDENT
Juvenile arrest

17) PERSON REPORTING CRIME OR INCIDENT
Det. J.Anderson

18) RES PHONE NO
266-4130

19) BUS PHONE NO.

22) RESIDENCE OF PERSON REPORTING CRIME or INCIDENT
OPD

23) LOCATION DISPATCHED TO
same as above

SECTOR #

24) TIME REPORTED
2121

25) DATE REPORTED
11-13-96

27) WAS FORCE USED
☐ YES ☒ NO ☐ UNKNOWN

29) STRANGER TO STRANGER
☐ YES ☐ NO ☐ UNKNOWN

28) WAS WEAPON USED
☐ YES ☒ NO ☐ UNKNOWN

30) HOW ATTACKED

31) TYPE OF PREMISES
Essex County Prosecutors Office

32) OBJECT OF ATTACK

33) MEANS OF ATTACK

34) MODUS OPERANDI

35) VEHICLE INVOLVED IN CRIME or INCIDENT
☐ STOLEN ☐ USED by OFFENDER ☐ INVOLVED

36) YEAR

37) MAKE

38) MODEL

39) LIC PLATE NO.

40) STATE

41) COLOR

42) SERIAL NO. Na

43) BODY TYPE

44) NAME OF SUBJECT OR MISSING PERSON STATE ALIAS IN BOX 55
Way,Nadir Kaseem

45) RESIDENCE
479 Union Avenue,Irvington,N.J.

46) SOCIAL SECURITY NO.

47) SEX	48) RACE	49) AGE	49A) DOB	49B) PLACE OF BIRTH	50) HEIGHT (INCHES)	51) WEIGHT	52) HAIR	53) EYES	54) CLOTHING WORN AND PECULIARITIES
M	blk	17	080879	N.J.	5'9"	140	brn	brn	

55) ADDITIONAL INFORMATION

Above named individual was arrested for 2C:11-3,2C:39-4 and 2C:39-5 in connection with an

incident that occurred at 325 Mechanic Street on Sunday,11-10-96,in particular the shooting

death of one Yafeu Fula age 19 of Whitier Place,East Orange.CC# 96-29039

The arrest took place at the offices of the Essex County Prosecutors Office in the New Court

Building in Newark.

62) PERSON ARRESTED
Way,Nadir Kaseem

63) ARREST NO.

64) PERSON ARRESTED

65) ARREST NO.

66) PERSON ARRESTED

67) ARREST NO.

68) PERSON ARRESTED

69) ARREST NO.

70) WITNESSES (NAME AND ADDRESS)

71) PHONE

72) TELETYPE NO.

73) DET. NOTIF

DEATHS SUICIDES

76) MEDICAL EXAMINER NOTIFIED

77) BODY WAS RELEASED BY PHONE ☐ PICKED UP ☐ NA

78) PRONOUNCED DEAD BY FOR HRS AT

AUTO THEFTS

79) RECOVERED AT

80) TIME

81) DATE

82) CAR TAKEN TO

83) VEHICLE PICKED UP BY

84) REPORTING OFFICER(S) SIGNATURE
Det.J.Anderson/

85) EMP. NO.
7

86) APPROVING SUPERVISORS SIGNATURE

87) EMP. NO.
516

Distribution: White – Records Bureau File   Pink – Desk Copy
Yellow – Detective or Investigation   Canary – Command Copy

VOLUNTARY STATEMENT OF SHARIF CLARK

Date: November 15, 1996
6 pages
Handwritten asterisks are from providing agency. Spelling corrections noted and initialed by Sharif Clark.

At the time of the shooting Sharif lived with his brother Rashad Clark, grandfather Ezra Clark, aunt Lois Beale, and sister Sameerah Clark at 23 Naden Avenue.

Sharif states he does not remember speaking to anyone on the phone Sunday morning after the shooting. Witness Lavie Johnson's statement on November 11, 1996 indicates she spoke with Sharif on the phone.

Sharif states he found out about the shooting from the paper and nobody in his family told him what occurred regarding the shooting.

Sharif states he did not know his brother confessed to shooting Yaki.

He knows his brother is in the Youth House but does not know why he is there.

Sharif does not know his brother Rashad's middle name.

| DATE: 11/15/96 | TIME: 1823 hrs. | PLACE: ESSEX COUNTY PROSECUTOR'S OFFICE | FILE NO: HOM122-96 |

VOLUNTARY STATEMENT OF:
Sharif Waleed Clark

AGE: 20 yrs.old

RESIDENCE:
23 Naden Avenue, Irvington

PHONE: 375-2341

| OCCUPATION | EMPLOYER: unemployed |

STATEMENT MADE TO:
Inv. Howard Johnson Essex County Prosecutor's Office

I am Investigator Howard Johnson of the Essex County Prosecutor's Office. I would like to ask you some questions regarding events surrounding the shooting of Yafeu A. Fula.

Q. Would you answer my questions?
A. Yeah.

Q. What is your date of birth, and your social security number?
A. 04/18/76. I don't know that.

Q. How long have you lived at your present address?
A. Fifteen years probably.

Q. Where did you live before 23 Naden Avenue?
A. I only lived there.

Q. Would you tell me everyone who lives in your house, and their relationship to you?
A. My grandfather, Ezra Clark, my aunt, Lois Beal, my sister, Sameerah Clark, my brother Rashad Clark, and me.

Q. Are you sure that no one else lives there?
A. Yeah that's it.

Q. How many telephone numbers are in your house? *Read aloud WRM 11-15-96*
A. Two.

Q. What are the two telephone numbers?
A. 375-2341, and 375-3893.

Q. Who has access to the telephones?
A. Just my family.

Q. Do you remember what occurred late Saturday night, November 09, 1996, leading into the early morning hours of Sunday November 10, 1996?
A. I was at my uncle's house, we was watching the Tyson/Holyfield fight. Me and my grandfather were a little drunk. After the fight my grandfather took me, and my brother home. I was knocked out on one couch, and my brother was on the other couch watching T.V.

Q. Which brother was with you watching the fight?
A. Roddy. Me, Roddy, and my grandfather.

Q. Who's house were you, and Roddy watching the fight at?
A. My uncle's house.

Q. Where does your uncle live, and what is his name?

SWORN AND SUBSCRIBED TO BEFORE ME THIS

_15_ DAY OF _Nov._ 19_96_   _Sharif Clark_
                                SIGNATURE

THIS AFFIDAVIT TAKEN PURSUANT TO CHAPTER 39 OF THE LAWS OF 1953

DATE: 11/15/96	TIME: 1823 hrs.	PLACE: ESSEX COUNTY PROSECUTOR'S OFFICE	FILE NO. HOM122-96

VOLUNTARY STATEMENT OF: Sharif Waleed Clark	AGE: 20 yrs.old

RESIDENCE: 23 Naden Avenue, Irvington	PHONE: 375-2341

OCCUPATION:	EMPLOYER: unemployed

STATEMENT MADE TO: Inv. Howard Johnson Essex County Prosecutor's Office

A. Where he live at umm, West Avon, in Irvington. Waleed Clark. He's a Corrections Officer at Northern State Prison.

Q. Did you or your brother leave your house after the Tyson fight?
A. Naw.

Q. Both you and Roddy, were at your house in the morning, after the Tyson Fight?
A. When I woke up, it was me my sister, and my niece, my aunt, and my grandfather. I didn't see Roddy since that night. When I woke up in the morning I didn't see him.

Q. Do you know where Roddy went?
A. Naw.

Q. Do you know if Roddy went to his girlfriend's house?
A. Naw, I was sleep. I didn't even talk to him after the fight.

Q. Did you wake up that night?
A. Naw.

Q. After you fell asleep on Sunday morning November 10, 1996, what time did you wake up Sunday morning?
A. I woke up in the afternoon time.

Q. When was the next time that you saw Roddy?
A. I haven't seen him since.

Q. Did you call anyone on the telephone that Sunday morning, November 10, 1996?
A. Naw, I didn't call anybody.

Q. Did you speak to anyone on the telephone Sunday morning, between the hours of 0300 a.m., and 0600 a.m., on November 10, 1996?
A. Naw, not that I remember.

Q. Have you ever seen your brother Roddy with a gun?
A. Naw.

Q. What time did you, Roddy, and your grandfather go to your uncle Waleed Clark's house to watch the Tyson/Holyfield fight?
A. It was around the eight round when we got there.

Q. Was Tyson, and Holyfield fighting?
A. Yeah.

Q. Did you stay to see the end of the fight?
A. Yeah.

SWORN AND SUBSCRIBED TO BEFORE ME THIS

_15_ DAY OF _NOV_ 19 _96_   _Sharif Clark_
SIGNATURE

THIS AFFIDAVIT TAKEN PURSUANT TO CHAPTER 39 OF THE LAWS OF 1953

DATE 11/15/96	TIME 1823 hrs.	PLACE ESSEX COUNTY PROSECUTOR'S OFFICE	FILE NO HOM122-96
VOLUNTARY STATEMENT OF: Sharif Waleed Clark			AGE 20 yrs.old
RESIDENCE 23 Naden Avenue, Irvington			PHONE 375-2341
OCCUPATION	EMPLOYER unemployed		
STATEMENT MADE TO: Inv. Howard Johnson Essex County Prosecutor's Office			

Q. Was Roddy there with you?
A. Yeah.

Q. Do you remember what you were wearing that night?
A. Umm, yeah Saturday a week ago, yeah. I had on a black shirt, my blue jeans, and the boots I'm wearing now.

Q. Do you remember what your brother Roddy was wearing?
A. Naw.

Q. How did you find out that Yafeu Fula was shot?
A. Paper.

✳ Q. Did anyone in your family tell you what occurred regarding the shooting?
A. Naw.

Q. Do you know Lavie Johnson from Orange?
A. Naw.

Q. Do you know Taalibah, from Orange?
A. Naw, I don't know Taalibah.

Q. Do you know Keisha?
A. Naw. I only be in Irvington, or Newark.

Q. Did you talk to anyone early Sunday morning?
A. I was asleep, I was drunk. Naw I didn't talk to nobody Sunday.

Q. Do you know where your brother Roddy is now?
A. In the Youth House.

Q. Do you know why your brother is in the Youth House?
A. Naw.

Q. What is Roddy's full name?
A. Rashad Clark.

Q. What is your brother's middle name?
A. I don't know. I don't know him like that.

Q. Are you known by any other name?
A. Naw.

Q. Are you aware that your brother was here yesterday, with his attorney, and that he confessed to shooting Yafeu?

SWORN AND SUBSCRIBED TO BEFORE ME THIS

___15___ DAY OF ___Nov___ 19_96_   _Sharif Clark_
                                     SIGNATURE

Robert H. Carell
THIS AFFIDAVIT TAKEN PURSUANT TO CHAPTER 39 OF THE LAWS OF 1953

DATE	TIME	PLACE	FILE NO.
11/15/96	1823 hrs.	ESSEX COUNTY PROSECUTOR'S OFFICE	HOM122-96

VOLUNTARY STATEMENT OF	AGE
Sharif Waleed Clark	20 yrs.old

RESIDENCE	PHONE
23 Naden Avenue, Irvington	375-2341

OCCUPATION	EMPLOYER
	unemployed

STATEMENT MADE TO
Inv. Howard Johnson Essex County Prosecutor's Office

A. Naw.

Q. Is this the first time that you learned that your brother Roddy shot Yafeu?
A. Yeah.

Q. Do you have any relatives that live in East Orange?
A. I don't know about that.

Q. Do you know Muta Beale?
A. Yeah.

Q. How do you know Mr. Beale?
A. That's my cousin.

Q. When was the last time that you saw Mr. Beale?
A. I have no idea. I've only been out of jail for three months.

Q. Do you know where Mr. Beale lives?
A. I Atlanta somewhere.

Q. Do you know what Mr. Beale does for a living?
A. He Raps. He rapped with Yafeu.

Q. Do you remember what Roddy was watching on the television just before you went to sleep?
A. Naw.

Q. Do you remember what time it was when you, Roddy, and your grandfather returned from watching the fight?
A. Naw. It was as soon as they was talking to Tyson, we was out of the door.

Q. From the time that you arrived home after watching the Tyson/Holyfield fight, until the time you woke up sometime Sunday afternoon. Did you speak to anyone from any telphone from within your house?
A. No.

Q. Do you know if anyone used the telephone early Sunday morning?
A. Oh naw, I don't know.

Q. Do you know someone named Taalibah?
A. Yeah, I got a cousin named Taalibah.

Q. What is Taalibah's full name, and where does she live?
A. I don't know her full name, I don't really mess with them.

Q. When was the last time that you heard from Taalibah?
A. Maybe about yesterday. She called my house for my grandfather.

SWORN AND SUBSCRIBED TO BEFORE ME THIS

___15___ DAY OF ___NOV___ 19_96_   _Sharif Clark_
SIGNATURE

THIS AFFIDAVIT TAKEN PURSUANT TO CHAPTER 39 OF THE LAWS OF 1953

DATE: 11/15/96	TIME: 1823 hrs.	PLACE: ESSEX COUNTY PROSECUTOR'S OFFICE	FILE NO. HOM122-96

VOLUNTARY STATEMENT OF: Sharif Waleed Clark	AGE: 20 yrs.old

RESIDENCE: 23 Naden Avenue, Irvington	PHONE: 375-2341

OCCUPATION:	EMPLOYER: unemployed

STATEMENT MADE TO:
Inv. Howard Johnson Essex County Prosecutor's Office

Q. Did you and Taalibah speak?
A. Yeah.

Q. Did she tell you anything about the shooting of Yafeu?
A. Naw. The only thing that I talked to her about is my grandfather, and I said he ain't here, and that was that.

Q. Do you know who would want to harm Yafeu?
A. Naw.

Q. How long did you know Yafeu?
A. Not long, about a month. I didn't really know him.

Q. What was the relationship between Yafeu, and Roddy?
A. I don't know.

Q. Did Yafeu every come over your house to visit Roddy?
A. Naw, not that I know of. No.

Q. Were Roddy, and Yafeu close friends?
A. I don't know.

Q. What was the last formal school that you attended?
A. Irvington High.

Q. What is the highest grade that you completed?
A. Eleventh.

Q. Can you read, write, and understand the English language?
A. Yeah.

Q. Is there anything else that you wish to add to your statement?
A. Naw.

Q. Have any threats, or promises been made to you for you to give this statement?
A. Naw.

Q. Do you swear, or affirm that the information which you just provided is the whole truth, and you do so under penalty of the law?
A. Yes.

Q. At the conclusion of your statement, would you read it, and make corrections, and when you are satisfied that it contains exactly what you have said. Would you sign your statement?
A. Alright.

SWORN AND SUBSCRIBED TO BEFORE ME THIS

_15_ DAY OF _Nov_ , 19 _96_ *Sharif Clark*
SIGNATURE

THIS AFFIDAVIT TAKEN PURSUANT TO CHAPTER 39 OF THE LAWS OF 1953

OFFICE OF THE ESSEX COUNTY PROSECUTOR

DATE: 11/15/96	**TIME:** 1823 hrs.	**PLACE:** ESSEX COUNTY PROSECUTOR'S OFFICE	**FILE NO:** HOM122-96

AGE: 20 yrs.old

VOLUNTARY STATEMENT OF:
Sharif Waleed Clark

PHONE: 375-2341

RESIDENCE:
23 Naden Avenue, Irvington

OCCUPATION:

EMPLOYER: unemployed

STATEMENT MADE TO:
Inv. Howard Johnson Essex County Prosecutor's Office

Q. Does Roddy belong to a gang?
A. No.

Q. Did Roddy see the last Tyson fight in Las Vegas?
A. No.

Q. Have you been receiving any threats from any gangs, or anyone?
A. I don't know who its' from. It ain't from no gang, its' from people.

Q. Mr. Clark before we conclude this statement, I would like to ask just a few more questions. Do you know Nadir Way?
A. Yeah.

Q. How do you know him?
A. He lives in my neighborhood.

Q. Does your brother Roddy, know Nadir Way?
A. I guess so.

Q. What is the relationship between your brother Roddy, and Nadir Way?
A. I don't know, they could be gay.

Q. Have you ever seen Roddy, and Nadir Way together before?
A. Naw.

Q. Do you know if your brother Roddy, and Nadir Way were together on Sunday, November 10, 1996?
A. Naw, I don't know.
Statement ended at 2011 hours on November 15, 1996...

SWORN AND SUBSCRIBED TO BEFORE ME THIS

15 DAY OF NOV 19 96   _Sharif Clark_
                                        SIGNATURE

THIS AFFIDAVIT TAKEN PURSUANT TO CHAPTER 39 OF THE LAWS OF 1953

THIS PAGE INTENTIONALLY LEFT BLANK

VOLUNTARY STATEMENT OF SAMUEL ROGERS

Date: November 16, 1996
4 pages
Redactions within statement made by publisher to protect personal information. Handwritten asterisks are from providing agency.

Rogers recognizes the detective as the one who investigated his own son's murder.

He mentions that he knows Yaasmyn Fula but not her son.

He is related to Rashad by marriage. Rogers' wife is the sister of Rashad's late mother.

He states in the early morning hours of 11/10/96, between 3:30 and 4:00am, Rashad and Kaseem came to his home.

Rashad said he had just had an argument with his baby's mother and he just left her house. While at Rogers' home, they called a cab and left. They stayed 15 – 20 minutes.

DATE:	TIME:	PLACE:		FILE NUMBER:
NOV. 16,1996	12:33PM	ESSEX CO. PROSECUTOR'S HOMICIDE SQUAD		H#122-96

VOLUNTARY STATEMENT OF:
SAMUEL ROGERS   SS# ▮▮▮▮▮▮▮▮▮

AGE: 57YRS
2-25-39

RESIDENCE:
92 SANFORD STREET   E. ORANGE, N.J.

PHONE:
266-1408

OCCUPATION:
UNEMPLOYED

EMPLOYER:

STATEMENT MADE TO:
DET. TIM BRAUN ESSEX CO. PROSECUTOR'S HOMICIDE SQUAD

Q. PLEASE STATE YOUR FULL NAME & CURRENT HOME ADDRESS ?
A. SMAUEL ROGERS 92 SANFORD STREET EAST ORANGE

Q. HOW LONG HAVE YOU LIVED AT 92 SANFORD STREET ?
A. JUST GOING ON 4 YEARS

Q. WHO LIVES WITH YOU AT 92 SANFORD STREET ?
A. MY WIFE BETTY, HER DAUGHTERS TALIBAH BROWN HER REAL NAME
IS LISA, YOLANDA BROWN, AND THIER KIDS MADIAH BROWN AND YOLANDA'S
SON TAGI HE'S 8 YEARS OLD, AND MY BROTHER WILLIAM ROGERS.

Q. WHAT IS YOUR WIFE'S FULL NAME ?
A. JUNE E. ROGERS BUT EVERYBODY CALLS HER BETTY.

Q. DO YOU USE ANY OTHER NAMES OR ATTRIBUTES ?
A. NO

Q. WHEN & WHERE WERE YOU BORN ?
A. MACKLEBERRY, VA. 2-25-39

Q. WHAT IS THE EXTENT OF YOUR EDUCATION ?
A. 5th or 6th GRADE

Q. CAN YOU READ, WRITE, & UNDERSTAND THE ENGLISH LANGUAGE ?
A. I CAN'T READ THAT GOOD BUT I CAN UNDERSTAND, I GET BY.

Q. MR. ROGERS, DO YOU KNOW WHO I AM ?
A. SURE, YOU THE DETECTIVE THAT HAD MY SON NATES CASE WHEN HE
GOT MURDERED IN WESTSIDE PARK A FEW YEARS AGO.   THAT BOY GOT
LIFE.

Q. MR. ROGERS, I AM INVESTIGATING THE SUNDAY NOVEMBER 10,1996
MURDER OF YAFEU FULA WHICH OCCURRED IN THE EARLY MORNING HOURS
AT 325 MECHANIC STREET IN THE CITY OF ORANGE, NEW JERSEY. ARE
YOU WILLING TO ANSWER A FEW QUESTIONS PERTAINING TO THIS INCIDENT
?
A.YES.

Q. ARE YOU AWARE OF THE INCIDENT I AM REFFERRING TOO ?
A. YES

Q. DO YOU KNOW THE PERSON WHO WAS KILLED DURING THIS INCIDENT?
A. I DON'T KNOW HIM BUT I KNOW HIS MOTHER

Q. DO YOU RECALL WHAT YOU WERE DURING THE EARLY MORNING HOURS
OF LAST SUNDAY NOVEMBER 10,1996 ?
A. I WAS HOME ASLEEP.

Q. WHO ELSE WAS AT YOUR HOME DURING THIS TIME ?
A. EVERYBODY EXCEPT LISA, SHE SPENT THE NIGHT WITH HER
GIRLFRIEND.Q.
Q. DURING THE EARLY MORNING HOURS OF LAST SUNDAY DID YOU RECEIVE
A VISIT FROM ANYONE AT YOUR HOME ?
A. YES, IT SOMETIME BETWEEN 3:30AM-4:00AM MY NEPHEW RASHAD AND

SWORN TO AND SUBSCRIBED BEFORE ME THIS

11th ___ DAY OF November 1996   _Samuel Rogers_
                                                    SIGNATURE
Inv. X. Johnson

THIS AFFIDAVIT TAKEN PURSUANT TO
CHAPTER 36 OF THE LAWS OF 1983

P-3 - Plate #8

OFFICE OF THE PROSECUTOR OF ESSEX COUNTY   NEWARK, N.J.

DATE:	TIME:	PLACE:	FILE NUMBER:
NOV. 16,1996	12:33PM	ESSEX CO. PROSECUTOR'S HOMICIDE SQUAD	H#122-96

VOLUNTARY STATEMENT OF:

SAMUEL ROGERS	SS# ███████	AGE 57YRS 2-25-39

RESIDENCE:		PHONE:
92 SANFORD STREET E. ORANGE, N.J.		266-1408

OCCUPATION:	EMPLOYER:
UNEMPLOYED	

STATEMENT MADE TO:

DET. TIM BRAUN ESSEX CO. PROSECUTOR'S HOMICIDE SQUAD

A. HIS FRIEND KAS CAME OVER AND WAS RINGING THE BELL.

Q. WHAT IS RASHAD'S FULL NAME AND ADDRESS ?
A. RASHAD CLARKE HE LIVES AT 23 NADEN AVE. IN IRVINGTON

Q. WHAT IS YOUR RELATIONSHIP WITH RASHAD CLARKE ?
A. I JUST MARRIED HIS AUNT.   MY WIFE BETTY IS RASHAD'S DECEASED
MOTHERS SISTER

Q. DO YOU KNOW KASSEM'S FULL NAME & ADDRESS ?
A. NO, I DON'T KNOW

Q. CAN YOU DESCRIBE KASSEM ?
A. I KNOW HIM TO SEE HIM, I CALL HIM WHITE BOY CAUSE HE'S SO
LIGHT, HE ABOUT 5'8" MAYBE, MEDIUM BUILT, ABOUT 16.

Q. DO YOU RECALL WHAT RASHAD & KASSEM WERE WEARING WHEN THEY
CAME TO YOUR HOME SUNDAY MORNING ?
A. I JUST WOKE UP AND I WASN'T PAYING THAT MUCH ATTENTION.

Q. WHAT DID YOU DO WHEN THEY CAME TO YOUR HOME ?
A. THEY WOKE ME UP RINGING THE BELL, THEN I WENT TO MY BEDROOM
WINDOW AND YELLED OUT AND ASKED WHO WAS THERE.   IT WAS RASHAD,
SO I WENT DOWNSTAIRS AND LET THEM IN.   I ASKED HIM IF HE WANTED
TO SPENT THE NIGHT.   RASHAD SAID "THAT HE JUST HAD AN ARGUMENT
WITH HIS BABY'S MOTHER AND HE JUST LEFT HER HOUSE".   THEN
THEY WENT IN THE KITCHEN AND CALLED A CAB AND LEFT.   AFTER
THAT I WENT BACK TO BED.

Q. HOW LONG DID RASHAD AND HIS FRIEND KASSEM STAY AT YOUR HOME?
A. I'D SAY NO MORE THEN 15-20 MINUTES, CAUSE AFTER THEY CALLED
THE CAB THEY LEFT.

Q. DO YOU KNOW WHAT CAB COMPANY THEY CALLED TO YOUR HOME ?
A. IT WAS A GREEN CAR, I DON'T KNOW THE NAME

Q. AT THE TIME RASHAD AND KASSEM WERE AT YOUR HOME, WERE YOU
AWARE OF THE SHOOTING INCIDENT ?
A. NO, I DIDN'T HEAR ANYTHING UNTIL I GOT TO CHURCH THAT MORNING
BUT I DIDN'T KNOW THAT RASHAD WAS INVOLVED.   THEY ACT LIKE
NOTHING HAPPENED WHEN THEY WAS AT MY HOUSE, THEY JUST CALLED
THE CAB AND LEFT.

Q. WAS IT UNUSUAL FOR RASHAD TO COME TO YOUR HOME AT THAT HOUR?
A. YEAH, HE DON'T USUALLY COME BY THAT LATE

Q. WHEN DID YOU LEARN THAT RASHAD WAS INVOLVED WITH THIS INCIDENT
?
A. I THINK IT WAS WEDNESDAY MY WIFE TOLD ME THAT SHE GOT A CALL
FROM RASHAD'S BROTHER SHARIF AND HE TOLD HER THAT RASHAD WAS
INVOLVED.

Q. WERE YOU FURNISHED WITH ANY DETAILS ABOUT HOW RASHAD WAS
INVOLVED WITH THIS INCIDENT ?

SWORN TO AND SUBSCRIBED BEFORE ME THIS

16th DAY OF November, 96

Inv. H. Johnson

① _Samuel Rogers_
SIGNATURE

THIS AFFIDAVIT TAKEN PURSUANT TO
CHAPTER 20 OF THE LAWS OF 1983

Plate #8

OFFICE OF THE PROSECUTOR OF ESSEX COUNTY   NEWARK, N. J.

DATE:	TIME:	PLACE:	FILE NUMBER:
NOV. 16,1996	12:33PM	ESSEX CO. PROSECUTOR'S HOMICIDE SQUAD	H#122-96

VOLUNTARY STATEMENT OF:		AGE: 57YRS
SAMUEL ROGERS SS# ▓▓▓▓▓▓▓		2-25-39

RESIDENCE:	PHONE:
92 SANFORD STREET E. ORANGE, N.J.	266-1408

OCCUPATION:	EMPLOYER:
UNEMPLOYED	

STATEMENT MADE TO:

DET. TIM BRAUN ESSEX CO. PROSECUTOR'S HOMICIDE SQUAD

A. NO, SHE JUST SAID HE WAS INVOLVED.

Q. WHAT WAS RASHAD'S PHYSICAL APPEARENCE WHEN HE ARRIVED AT YOUR HOME SUNDAY MORNING ?
A. HE SEEMED NORMAL, LIKE NOTHING WAS WRONG WITH HIM

Q. DID RASHAD APPEAR TO UNDER THE INFLUENCE OF DRUGS OR ALCOHOL WHEN HE ARRIVED AT YOUR HOME ?
A. NO, I DON'T THINK SO

Q. DID KASSEM APPEAR TO BE UNDER THE INFLUENCE OF DRUGS OR ALCOHOL WHEN HE ARRIVED AT YOUR HOME ?
A. HE DIDN'T APPEAR LIKE NOTHING WAS WRONG WITH HIM

Q. DID YOU SEE KASSEM OR RASHAD WITH A GUN WHEN THEY WERE AT YOUR HOME ?
A. NO, I DIDN'T SEE KNOW GUNS

Q. HAVE YOU EVER SEEN RASHAD WITH A GUN ?
A. NO, I NEVER SEEN HIM WITH A GUN

Q. HAVE YOU EVER SEEN KASSEM WITH A GUN ?
A. NO

Q. HOW MANY TIMES HAS KASSEM BEEN TO YOUR HOME ?
A. PLENTY TIMES

Q. WHAT IS THE RELATIONSHIP BETWEEN RASHAD AND KASSEM ?
A. THEY FRIENDS, I KNOW THEY AIN'T NO KIN

Q. DO YOU KNOW IF RAHSAD AND YAFEU FULA ARE FRIENDS ?
A. I DON'T EVEN KNOW TO TELL YOU THE TRUTH.

Q. BESIDES YOURSELF, WAS ANYONE ELSE IN YOUR HOME AWAKEN WHEN RASHAD AND KASSEM CAME BY SUNDAY MORNING ?
A. NO, EXCEPT MY WIFE BUT SHE DIDN'T GET OUT OF BED.

Q. WHICH PHONE DID THEY USE TO CALL THE CAB ?
A. THE ONE IN THE KITCHEN

Q. HOW MANY PHONE NUMBERS DO YOU HAVE IN YOUR HOME ?
A. TWO, 266-1408 & 414-0836

Q. WHICH PHONE NUMBER DID THEY USE TO CALL THE CAB ?
A. 266-1408

Q. DO YOU KNOW WHO ACTUALLY CALLED THE CAB COMPANY ?
A. I DON'T KNOW, BUT I THINK RASHAD, THEY BOTH WENT IN THE KITCHEN AND I WAS IN THE LIVINGROOM ON THE SOFA.

Q. WOULD YOU RECOGNIZE A PHOTO OF RASHAD AND KASSEM IF YOU WERE TO SEE THEM AGAIN ?
A. YES

SWORN TO AND SUBSCRIBED BEFORE ME THIS

16th DAY OF November ,96

Inv. S. Johnson

(X) _Samuel Rogers_ (signature)
SIGNATURE

THIS AFFIDAVIT TAKEN PURSUANT TO
CHAPTER 310 OF THE LAWS OF 1953

- Plate #8

OFFICE OF THE PROSECUTOR OF ESSEX COUNTY   NEWARK, N. J.

DATE:	TIME:	PLACE:	FILE NUMBER:
NOV. 16.1996	12:33PM	ESSEX CO. PROSECUTOR'S HOMICIDE SQUAD	H#122-96

VOLUNTARY STATEMENT OF:
SAMUEL ROGERS   SS# ███████   AGE 57YRS   2-25-39

RESIDENCE:
92 SANFORD STREET   E. ORANGE, N.J.   PHONE: 266-1408

OCCUPATION: UNEMPLOYED   **EMPLOYER:**

STATEMENT MADE TO:
DET. TIM BRAUN ESSEX CO. PROSECUTOR'S HOMICIDE SQUAD

Q. COULD YOU PLEASE LOOK AT THIS ARRAY WHICH IS MARKED WITH
THE LETTER "A" AND TELL ME IF YOU RECOGNIZE ANYONE IN THE ARRAY?
A. NUMBER 3, THAT'S KASSEM BUT THAT'S A BAD PICTURE (NOTE:
WITNESS IDENTIFIES A PHOTO OF NADIR KASSEM WAY).

Q. IS THIS THE SAME PERSON YOU HAVE REFFERED TO AS KASSEM
THROUGHOUT THIS ENTIRE STATEMENT ?
A. YEAH, THAT'S THE ONE WHO WAS WITH RASHAD THE OTHER NIGHT.

Q. WILL YOU PLEASE SIGN AND DATE THE BACK OF THE PHOTO YOU HAVE
JUST IDENTIFIED ?
A. O.K. (WITNESS COMPLIES BY PLACING HIS SIGNATURE ON THE BACK
OF NADIR K. WAYS PHOTO).

Q. WOULD YOU PLEASE LOOK AT ANOTHER PHOTO THAT IS MARKED AS
ARRAY "B" AND TELL ME IF YOU RECOGNIZE ANYONE IN THIS ARRAY?
A. OH YEAH, NUMBER 4 THAT'S RASHAD (NOTE: WITNESS HAS IDENTIFIED
A PHOTO OF RASHAD CLARKE)

Q. IS THIS THE SAME PERSON WHO YOU REFFERED TO AS RASHAD
THROUGHOUT THIS ENTIRE STATEMENT ?
A. YES

Q. WILL YOU PLEASE SIGN AND DATE THE BACK OF THE PHOTO THAT
YOU HAVE JUST IDENTIFIED AS RASHAD ?
A. YES, (WITNESS COMPLIES BY PLACING HIS SIGNATURE ON THE BACK
OF PHOTO #4 OF ARRAY "B")

Q. IS THERE ANYTHING I HAVE NOT ASKED YOU THAT YOU WISH TO ADD
TO THIS STATEMENT ?
A. NO

Q. HAS EVERYTHING YOU STATED BEEN THE TRUTH TO THE BEST OF YOUR
KNOWLEDGE ?
A. YES

Q. HAVE YOU BEEN THREATENED OR PROMISED ANYTHING IN RETURN FOR
THIS STATEMENT ?
A. NO, AIN'T NOBODY THREATEN ME

Q. WOULD YOU LIKE TO HAVE THIS STATEMENT READ BACK TO YOU BY
DET. ARIC WEBSTER OF THE ORANGE POLICE ?
A. YES

Q. IF YOU FIND THAT DURING THE READING OF THIS STATEMENT THAT
YOU WANT TO MAKE A CORRECTION, PLEASE STOP AND MAKE THE
CORRECTION ?
A. O.K.

STATEMENT ENDED AT 1:46pm

SWORN TO AND SUBSCRIBED BEFORE ME THIS

16th DAY OF November, 96

Tim H. Johnson   X _Samuel Rogers_
SIGNATURE

THIS AFFIDAVIT TAKEN PURSUANT TO
CHAPTER 3 OF THE LAWS OF 1963

P-3 — Plate #8

THIS PAGE INTENTIONALLY LEFT BLANK

VOLUNTARY STATEMENT OF GARFIELD SHARPE

Date: November 15, 1996
4 pages
Redactions within statement made by publisher to protect personal information. Handwritten asterisks are from providing agency. Corrections noted and initialed by Garfield Sharpe.

Garfield Sharpe went to school with Yaki in Montclair.

Garfield states two days before the shooting, early Friday morning he saw Rashad who asked him where Yaki was. He told him Yaki was up the street. Garfield rode up the street and told Yaki.

Garfield states he does not know if Rashad was "pilled up" but every time he got up he was falling.

Yaki and Rashad were having a disagreement about money that Rashad was asking for.

Rashad told Yaki he did not like his "tall red ass."

They began arguing. Rashad told Yaki he was going to "kill him." Yaki responded "You couldn't kill a bug."

Rashad asked Yaki where he had his "gat." Yaki responded he did not have a "gat."

Rashad said he had "3 gats."

Garfield says Rashad made threats to kill Yaki to Lavie.

Garfield states Yaki had been wearing his bulletproof vest since September to help save his life.

DATE	TIME	PLACE	
11/15/96	1347 hrs.	ESSEX COUNTY PROSECUTOR'S OFFICE	FILE NO HOM122-96

VOLUNTARY STATEMENT OF:	AGE:
Garfield Ricardo Sharpe	19 yrs. old

RESIDENCE:	PHONE:
37 Tichenor Place, Montclair	746-9642

OCCUPATION	EMPLOYER:
student	Montclair High School

STATEMENT MADE TO:
Inv. Howard Johnson Essex County Prosecutor's Office

I am Investigator Howard Johnson of the Essex County Prosecutor's Office. I would like to ask you some questions regarding circumstances surrounding the death of Yafeu A. Fula.

Q. Would you answer my questions?
A. As best as I can.

Q. What is your date of birth, and your social security number?
A. 12/16/76. ████████

Q. How long have you lived at your present address?
A. About six, or seven years.

Q. Where did you live prior to your present address?
A. 12 Tichenor Place.

Q. Can you read, write, and understand the English language?
A. Yes, I could read, write, and understand the English language.

Q. What is the highest level of education that you have completed?
A. Eleventh, I'm in the twelfth now.

Q. Did you know Yafeu A. Fula?
A. Yes.

Q. How did you know Mr. Fula?
A. I went to school with him, and I also knew him from the streets.

Q. How long did you know Mr. Fula?
A. About six, or seven years.

Q. How did you learn of Mr. Fula's death?
A. I heard it from a friend on Sunday morning.

Q. Do you know of an argument which occurred prior to the shooting of Mr. Fula?
A. Yeah, about two days before the shooting, early Friday morning, I was riding on a bike, and I came up to the Exxon gas station on Bloomfield Avenue. I seen "Roddy", he asked me where "Yaf", and "Fatal" was at. I told him that was up the street. He told me that if I seen "Fatal", to tell "Fatal" to make him a tape. I told him to wait right here, and went up the street to tell "Fatal", but "Fatal" was up the street, so I told "Yaf". Umm, "Yaf" asked me where was "Roddy" at, I told him that he was at the Exxon. Umm, Yafeu asked me if he could borrow my bike, and I told him yes. He rode to umm, down the street to Exxon, and I was behind him. When he got to the Exxon, "Roddy" asked him to make him a tape. He told "Roddy" naw, I can't do it right now. Roddy was sitting on a milk crate, and Yafeu was sitting right next to him at the Exxon right by the garbage. Roddy was rolling up a "black and mild cigar, and Yaf was telling him come on the mild was all wet. I don't know if Roddy was "pilled up", or "doped up", but every time that he got up he was falling. They started talking, and Roddy asked

SWORN AND SUBSCRIBED TO BEFORE ME THIS

_15th_ DAY OF _NOVEMBER_ 96   _Garfield Sharpe_
                                    SIGNATURE

LT. S.A. Cruz
THIS AFFIDAVIT TAKEN PURSUANT TO CHAPTER 39 OF THE LAWS OF 1953

DATE 11/15/96	TIME 1347 hrs.	PLACE ESSEX COUNTY PROSECUTOR'S OFFICE	FILE NO HOM122-96
VOLUNTARY STATEMENT OF Garfield Ricardo Sharpe			AGE 19 yrs. old
RESIDENCE 37 Tichenor Place, Montclair			PHONE 746-9642
OCCUPATION student		EMPLOYER Montclair High School	
STATEMENT MADE TO Inv. Howard Johnson Essex County Prosecutor's Office			

Yaf how much money was he going to give him, and Yaf answered, "I told you that I was going to give you a hundred dollars. Roddy replied, and said, "what you mean you going to give me a hundred dollars", and Yaf replied a hundred, a hundred, just like I said. In the process of this Roddy was telling Yafeu that he didn't like his tall red ass. When they was arguing Roddy was saying that I'm going to kill you, I'm going to kill you to Yaf, and Yaf said, "you couldn't kill a bug". Roddy said that I got the "gat" on me right now, and Yaf said that he didn't care if he had thirty "gats". Roddy said to Yaf, where's your "gat" at, and Yaf said he didn't have a "gat". Roddy said something like he had three "gats" of his own Within all this arguing and everything, I told Yaf come on let's get him up out of here before the police come, and Yaf said come on Roddy you got to go, and Roddy said I'm ~~alright~~. Roddy was saying let's go to Keisha's house, and Yaf didn't really reply.
alright

Q. Do you know Roddy's real name?
A. No I do not.

Q. How long have you known Roddy?
A. I didn't know Roddy personally, I just know him from Yaf, and Bruce introducing him to me.

Q. Do you know where Roddy lives?
A. Somewhere in Irvington, I think.

Q. Have you ever seen Roddy with a gun?
A. No.

Q. What is a "gat"?
A. A short definition of a gun, used on the street.

Q. What time, and date did Roddy, and Yafeu argue?
A. About early Friday morning, a couple of days before Yafeu was shot.

Q. Who is "Fatal"?
A. Bruce Washington, and he is a member of Death Row Records. He's probably Yafeu's best friend.

Q. Do you know where Bruce Washington lives?
A. No.

Q. What is a black, and mild cigar?
A. It's a cigar.

Q. Do you know why Roddy threatened to kill Yafeu?
A. I really don't know.

Q. Do you know if Roddy belongs to any gang, or has affiliation with any gang?
A. I don't know.

Q. Did anyone else hear the threat by Roddy, on Yafeu's life?

SWORN AND SUBSCRIBED TO BEFORE ME THIS

_15th_ DAY OF _NOVEMBER_ 19_96_   SIGNATURE _____

LT. S.R. C____

THIS AFFIDAVIT TAKEN PURSUANT TO CHAPTER 39 OF THE LAWS OF 1953

DATE	TIME:	PLACE	FILE NO.
11/15/96	1347 hrs.	ESSEX COUNTY PROSECUTOR'S OFFICE	HOM122-96

VOLUNTARY STATEMENT OF:	AGE
Garfield Ricardo Sharpe	19 yrs. old

RESIDENCE	PHONE:
37 Tichenor Place, Montclair	746-9642

OCCUPATION	EMPLOYER
student	Montclair High School

STATEMENT MADE TO:
Inv. Howard Johnson Essex County Prosecutor's Office

A. No, just me and Yafeu.

Q. Do you know if Yafeu told Bruce Washington, or anyone else about the threat on his life?
A. I don't know.

Q. Do you know if anyone else wanted to harm Yafeu?
A. I really don't know. I really couldn't answer you.

Q. Do you know of any threats that were made to Lavie Johnson, towards Yafeu?
A. Yeah, Roddy was making threats to kill Yafeu to Lavie.

Q. Do you know when the threats took place?
A. Maybe like a couple of weeks before he was killed.

Q. Do you know why Yafeu was wearing a bullet proof vest?
A. To help save his life, I guess.

Q. Do you know how long Yafeu was wearing a bullet proof vest?
A. I know that Bruce Washington wore his vest a lot, and Yafeu was wearing his vest at least since September.

Q. Do you know a man named Muta?
A. I don't him by Muta, I know a Muta Beals.

Q. Where does Muta Beals live?
A. I heard that he lives in Irvington.

Q. Do you know if Muta knows Yafeu?
A. Yes, Muta knows Yafeu.

Q. What is the relationship between Muta, and Yafeu?
A. Muta is also a member of Death Row Records.

Q. Do you know if Muta knows Roddy?
A. They are cousins.

Q. Do you wish to add anything else to you statement?
A. No I do not. Not at this time.

Q. Have any threats, or promises been made to you, for you to give this statement?
A. No, not at all.

Q. Do you swear, or affirm that the information which you have just provided, is the whole truth, and you do so under penalty of the law?
A. Yes.

SWORN AND SUBSCRIBED TO BEFORE ME THIS

15TH DAY OF NOVEMBER 1996   _Garfield Sharpe_
                               SIGNATURE

LT. SR _____
THIS AFFIDAVIT TAKEN PURSUANT TO CHAPTER 19 OF THE LAWS OF 1953

OFFICE OF THE ESSEX COUNTY PROSECUTOR

NEWARK, NJ

DATE	TIME	PLACE	FILE NO
11/15/96	1347 hrs.	ESSEX COUNTY PROSECUTOR'S OFFICE	HOM122-96

VOLUNTARY STATEMENT OF:	AGE
Garfield Ricardo Sharpe	19 yrs. old

RESIDENCE	PHONE
37 Tichenor Place, Montclair	746-9642

OCCUPATION	EMPLOYER
student	Montclair High School

STATEMENT MADE TO
Inv. Howard Johnson   Essex County Prosecutor's Office

Q. At the conclusion of your statement, would you read, make any corrections, and when you are satisfied that it contains exactly what you have told me, would you sign your statement?

A. Yes if its' correct.

Statement ended at 0333 hours, on 11/15/96...

THIS PAGE INTENTIONALLY LEFT BLANK

REQUEST FOR EXAMINATION OF FIREARM EVIDENCE

Date: November 18, 1996
1 page

Crime: Homicide

Suspects: Nadir Way and Rashaad Clarke (sic)

Victim shot in the face while standing in hallway of 325 Mechanic Street, Orange, NJ.

Lead projectile recovered from Yaki's head at autopsy.

OFFICE OF THE SHERIFF
ARMANDO B. FONTOURA, Sheriff
ESSEX COUNTY COURTS BUILDING
NEWARK, NEW JERSEY 07102
(201) 621-4111

BALLISTICS...x4085

REQUEST FOR EXAMINATION OF FIREARM EVIDENCE

Crime: HOMICIDE	Date of Incident: NOVEMBER 10,1996	Lab No.:(leave blank) 96-6462
Victim(s): YAFEU FULA	Suspect(s): NADIR WAY & RASHAAD CLARKE	

Submitting Agency: (include address) ESSEX CO. PROSECUTOR'S HOMICIDE SQUAD	Case No.: HOMICIDE #122-96
Forward replies to: DET. TIM BRAUN E.C.P.O. HOMICIDE SQUAD	Telephone No.: (201)621-4318
Investigated by: DET. TIM BRAUN	Person Delivering Evidence:(sign & print) DET. TIM BRAUN 11-18-96

Brief History of Case: (include date & location, if applicable)
ON NOVEMBER 10,1996 AT APPROXIMATELY 3:40AM THE VICTIM WAS SHOT ONCE IN THE FACE WHILE STANDING IN THE HALLWAY OF 325 MECHANIC STREET ORANGE,N.J. AT THIS STAGE OF THE INVESTIGATION A MOTIVE HAS NOT BEEN ESTABLISHED, ALTHOUGH TWO SUSPECTS HAVE BEEN ARRESTED AND CHARGED WITH THE KILLING.

Examination Requested: (on specimens listed below)

___ Test for Operability   XX Input into "IBIS"

___ Attempt to Restore Serial Numbers

XX Identify/Microscopically Compare   ___ Other: _____

LIST OF SPECIMENS* (only one firearm per page/lab #)

Item#	Code**	
1	VIC	LEAD PROJECTILE RECOVERED FROM THE VICTIMS HEAD AT HIS AUTOPSY.

*list firearms (caliber/type/make/model/serial number)
**source, Code for evidence (v=victim, s=suspect, sc=scene)

Received by:(chain of custody)	Agency/Title: ESSEX COUNTY SHERIFF'S OFFICE	Date: 11-18-96
Returned by:	Agency/Title: ESSEX COUNTY SHERIFF'S OFFICE	Date:
Received by:(sign & print)	Agency/Title:	Date:

rev.9/96   ATTACH EXTRA PAGES IF NEEDED   Page ___ of ___

VOLUNTARY STATEMENT OF SAMEERAH TURNER

Date: November 18, 1996
7 pages
Handwritten notes are from providing agency.

Sameerah Turner is the mother of Rashad Clark's daughter, Shantel Shateerah Turner.

Sameerah stopped seeing Rashad romantically two months prior.

She sold Rashad's pager but does not recall who she sold it to.

She does not recall the last time she spoke to Rashad.

Sameerah denies seeing or speaking to Rashad or his family since the shooting. This contradicts the statement of her mother Brenda Turner, who stated Rashad's sister came to pick up Sameerah and family members were calling her house after the shooting.

Brenda Turner further stated Sameerah told her Rashad said gunpowder was all over him and he took everything off and went to different people's houses where he was given clothing. When the police came to Rashad's house requesting his clothing, Rashad's family asked Sameerah to go get his clothing, which she did.

Sameerah denied picking up clothing at different locations.

Brenda Turner stated after the shooting her daughter started getting money from Rashad's family. She stated the family did not previously care about the health and welfare of Sameerah and her granddaughter and that their interest just started, but it stopped when they found out Sameerah had given a statement to the prosecutor's office.

OFFICE OF THE ESSEX COUNTY PROSECUTOR

DATE: 11/18/96	TIME: 1737 hrs.	PLACE: ESSEX COUNTY PROSECUTOR'S OFFICE	NEWARK, NJ

FILE NO: HOM122-96

VOLUNTARY STATEMENT OF:
Sameerah Wajaeerah Turner

AGE: 16 yrs. old

RESIDENCE:
27 Wilson Place, 2nd floor, Irvington

PHONE: 372-1377

OCCUPATION: Student   **EMPLOYER:** Irvington High School (Nights)

STATEMENT MADE TO:
Inv. Howard Johnson   Essex County Prosecutor's Office

I am Investigator Howard Johnson of the Essex County Prosecutor's Office. I would like to ask you some questions regarding events surrounding the shooting of Yafeu A. Fula.

Q. Would you answer my questions?
A. Yeah.

Q. What is your date of birth, and your social security number?
A. Umm, July 28, 1980. I don't know my social security number.

Q. How long have you lived at your present address?
A. I don't know.

Q. Where did you live prior to your current address?
A. 248 Munn Avenue, Irvington.

Q. Who resides with you at your current address?
A. I don't know.

Q. Can you read, write and understand the English language?
A. Umm huh.

Q. What was the highest grade that you completed?
A. Eleventh.

Q. Do you know **Rashad Clark**?
A. Yeah.

Q. How long have you known Rashad Clark?
A. For like a year.

Q. What is your relationship to Rashad Clark?
A. Baby father.

Q. What is your baby's name?
A. Shantel Shateerah Turner.

Q. How old is your child?
A. Two months.

Q. Are you and Rashad still seeing each other romantically?
A. No.

Q. When did you stop seeing Rashad romantically?
A. Two months ago.

SWORN AND SUBSCRIBED TO BEFORE ME THIS

18th DAY OF November, 1996

SIGNATURE

THIS AFFIDAVIT TAKEN PURSUANT TO CHAPTER 39 OF THE LAWS OF 1953

DATE	TIME	PLACE	
11/18/96	1737 hrs.	ESSEX COUNTY PROSECUTOR'S OFFICE	FILE NO. HOM122-96

VOLUNTARY STATEMENT OF: Sameerah Wajaeerah Turner	AGE 16 yrs. old

RESIDENCE: 27 Wilson Place, 2nd floor, Irvington	PHONE 372-1377

OCCUPATION: Student	EMPLOYER: Irvington High School (Nights)

STATEMENT MADE TO:
Inv. Howard Johnson   Essex County Prosecutor's Office

Q. What do you call Rashad Clark?
A. Roddy.

Q. Where did the two of you meet?
A. At school.

Q. Did the two of you have an exclusive relationship?
A. Yeah.

Q. When was the last time that you saw Rashad Clark?
A. Like, last week some time.

Q. Do you remember what day it was when you saw Rashad?
A. Nope.

Q. Did you see him during the middle of the week, or towards the end of last week?
A. I forgot.

Q. Was your daughter with you when you saw Rashad?
A. Um huh.

Q. Where did you see Rashad, what location were you at?
A. His house.

Q. Do you know where Rashad is at this moment?
A. Yeah, at the Youth House.

Q. Have you spoken to Rashad since he was arrested?
A. No.

Q. Have you spoken to anyone in Rashad's family since Rashad was arrested?
A. Just his sister.

Q. What is Rashad's sister's name?
A. Sameerah Clark.

Q. Where does Sameerah Clark live?
A. I don't know.

Q. Do you have Rashad Clark's pager?
A. No.

Q. Where is the pager?
A. I sold it.

SWORN AND SUBSCRIBED TO BEFORE ME THIS

18th DAY OF November 19 96

SIGNATURE

THIS AFFIDAVIT TAKEN PURSUANT TO CHAPTER 49 OF THE LAWS OF 1953

OFFICE OF THE ESSEX COUNTY PROSECUTOR

NEWARK, NJ

| DATE: 11/18/96 | TIME: 1737 hrs. | PLACE: ESSEX COUNTY PROSECUTOR'S OFFICE | FILE NO HOM122-96 |

| VOLUNTARY STATEMENT OF: Sameerah Wajaeerah Turner | AGE: 16 yrs. old |

| RESIDENCE: 27 Wilson Place, 2nd floor, Irvington | PHONE: 372-1377 |

| OCCUPATION: Student | EMPLOYER: Irvington High School (Nights) |

STATEMENT MADE TO:
Inv. Howard Johnson   Essex County Prosecutor's Office

Q. Who did you sell the pager to?
A. I don't know. What I need a pager for, and I got my own pager.

Q. What was the number to the pager?
A. 905-2850.

Q. What area code is that pager number?
A. (201)

Q. Did Rashad's sister Sameerah pick you up from your home, on Tuesday, or Wednesday of last week?
A. No.

Q. Did Rashad's aunt pick you up last week?
A. No.

Q. Did you ride in a Neon last week?
A. Yeah.

Q. Who was driving that car?
A. My sister.

Q. What is your sister's name?
A. Jameeyah Tuner.

Q. Has anyone questioned you regarding, what Rashad said to you about the shooting?
A. No.

Q. Has anyone told you how to respond to these questions?
A. No. Sir.

Q. Did you spend some time with Rashad last week?
A. No.

Q. Did you see Rashad last week?
A. No.

Q. When was the last time that you have spoken to Rashad Clark?
A. I forgot.

Q. Did you speak to Rashad on Monday, or Tuesday of last week?
A. No.

Q. Did you speak to Rashad on Wednesday, or Thursday of last week?
A. No Sir.

SWORN AND SUBSCRIBED TO BEFORE ME THIS

_18_ DAY OF _November_ 19_96_   SIGNATURE

THIS AFFIDAVIT TAKEN PURSUANT TO CHAPTER 39 OF THE LAWS OF 1955

Page 3

DATE 11/18/96	TIME 1737 hrs.	PLACE ESSEX COUNTY PROSECUTOR'S OFFICE	FILE NO. HOM122-96

VOLUNTARY STATEMENT OF: Sameerah Wajaeerah Turner		AGE 16 yrs. old

RESIDENCE 27 Wilson Place, 2nd floor, Irvington	PHONE 372-1377

OCCUPATION Student	EMPLOYER Irvington High School (Nights)

STATEMENT MADE TO: Inv. Howard Johnson Essex County Prosecutor's Office

Q. Did you speak to Rashad on Friday, or Saturday of last week?
A. No.

Q. When was the last time that you spoke to someone from Rashad Clark's family?
A. Umm, I forgot.

Q. Did you speak to someone from Rashad's family today?
A. No.

Q. Did you speak to someone from Rashad's family yesterday, Sunday November 17, 1996?
A. No.

Q. Did you speak to anyone in Rashad's family either Wednesday, or Thursday November 13, or 14, 1996?
A. No.

Q. Has any family member from Rashad's home located at 23 Naden Street, in Irvington called you?
A. No.

Q. Are you saying that no family member of Rashad Clark's has contacted you prior to his arrest last week?
A. That's how I found out that he was arrested.

Q. So no one has contacted you from Rashad's family since they contacted you regarding Rashad's arrest?
A. No.

Q. Did you speak to Detective Noel, from the Irvington Police Department, last week?
A. Yeah.

Q. What did you speak to her about?
A. I hung up on her.

Q. Why were you involved with the Irvington Police Department?
A. My mother, that's all I know.

Q. Do you remember what day of the week that was?
A. Nope.

Q. Where were you when you spoke to Detective Noel?
A. At that boy's house, Lameesh.

Q. Where does Lameesh live?
A. I forgot.

Q. What is Lameesh's full name?
A. I don't know.

SWORN AND SUBSCRIBED TO BEFORE ME THIS

18th DAY OF November 96

SIGNATURE

THIS AFFIDAVIT TAKEN PURSUANT TO CHAPTER 39 OF THE LAWS OF 1953

Page 4

DATE	TIME	PLACE	
11/18/96	1737 hrs.	ESSEX COUNTY PROSECUTOR'S OFFICE	FILE NO. HOM122-96

VOLUNTARY STATEMENT OF:	AGE
Sameerah Wajaeerah Turner	16 yrs. old

RESIDENCE:	PHONE
27 Wilson Place, 2nd floor, Irvington	372-1377

OCCUPATION	EMPLOYER
Student	Irvington High School (Nights)

STATEMENT MADE TO:
Inv. Howard Johnson Essex County Prosecutor's Office

Q. Where did you meet Lameesh ?
A. Like Springfield, and Styvesant.

Q. How many telephones are there in your home?
A. Two.

Q. What are the telephone numbers?
A. 372-1377, 372-6592.

Q. Which telephone line do you use most frequently?
A. Both of them.

Q. How often has Rashad been to your home?
A. Like a good fifty. Somewhere in there.

Q. Has his sister Sameerah been to your home, as well?
A. Umm, huh.

Q. Has Sameerah slept at your home?
A. Yeah.

Q. When was the last time that you have seen Sameerah Clark?
A. I forgot.

Q. Do you remember if you have seen her this past Saturday, or Sunday?
A. No, I don't remember.

Q. Do you remember speaking to Sameerah Clark this past weekend?
A. No.

Q. When was the last time that you spoke to Sameerah Clark?
A. Like three weeks ago.

Q. So you have not spoken to Sameerah Clark since about three weeks ago, is that right?
A. Yeah.

Q. Have any of Rashad's family members asked you to pick up any clothing at different locations?
A. No.

Q. Have you ever seen Rashad with a gun?
A. Nope.

Q. Do you know any of Rashad's friends?
A. Nope.

SWORN AND SUBSCRIBED TO BEFORE ME THIS

18th DAY OF November 19 96

SIGNATURE

THIS AFFIDAVIT TAKEN PURSUANT TO CHAPTER 19 OF THE LAWS OF 1953

| DATE 11/18/96 | TIME 1737 hrs. | PLACE ESSEX COUNTY PROSECUTOR'S OFFICE | FILE NO HOM122-96 |

VOLUNTARY STATEMENT OF:
Sameerah Wajaeerah Turner

AGE 16 yrs. old

RESIDENCE
27 Wilson Place, 2nd floor, Irvington

PHONE 372-1377

OCCUPATION
Student

EMPLOYER:
Irvington High School (Nights)

STATEMENT MADE TO:
Inv. Howard Johnson Essex County Prosecutor's Office

Q. Do you know Kas, a.k.a. Nadir Way?
A. Nope.

Q. Do you know where Rashad Clark lives?
A. Yeah, 23 Naden Avenue, Irvington.

Q. How many times have you been to Rashad's home?
A. I can't even tell you. A lot.

Q. Who lives at Rashad's home with Rashad?
A. His grandfather, his sister Sameerah, his brother Shariff, and his aunt , I call her nickname Miss Mackey, her real name is Miss Beale.

Q. Did you leave your home last week without your mother's permission?
A. Yeah.

Q. Where did you go?
A. I spent the night at Lameesh's house.

Q. During the time that you left home, did you see Rashad?
A. Nope.

Q. Did you take your baby to see Rashad prior to his arrest?
A. Yeah, before he turned himself in on Thursday.

Q. Where did you see Rashad, when he saw the baby, what location was it?
A. 23 Naden Avenue.

Q. Who was at 23 Naden Avenue when you saw Rashad?
A. Him, and his Lawyer, and his grandfather?

Q. Do you know who paid for Rashad's lawyer?
A. No.

Q. How does Roddy support himself?
A. His mother, and father passed. Social security.

Q. Did you see Roddy earlier that week, prior to his arrest?
A. No.

Q. Has any of Rashad's family or friends, coached you as to what to say during this statement?
A. No.

Q. Would you like to add anything else to you statement?

SWORN AND SUBSCRIBED TO BEFORE ME THIS
18th DAY OF November 96

SIGNATURE

THIS AFFIDAVIT TAKEN PURSUANT TO CHAPTER 39 OF THE LAWS OF 1953

DATE	TIME	PLACE	FILE NO.
11/18/96	1737 hrs.	ESSEX COUNTY PROSECUTOR'S OFFICE	HOM122-96

VOLUNTARY STATEMENT OF:	AGE:
Sameerah Wajaeerah Turner	16 yrs. old

RESIDENCE:	PHONE:
27 Wilson Place, 2nd floor, Irvington	372-1377

OCCUPATION:	EMPLOYER:
Student	Irvington High School (Nights)

STATEMENT MADE TO:
Inv. Howard Johnson   Essex County Prosecutor's Office

A. No Sir.

Q. Have any threats, or promises been made to you to give this statement?
A. No.

Q. Do you swear, or affirm that the information which you have just provided, is the whole truth, and you do so under penalty of the law?
A. Yes, I do.

Q. At the conclusion of this statement would you read it, make all corrections, and when you are satisfied that it contains exactly what you have told me, would you sign your statement?
A. Yeah.

Statement ended at 1957 hours, on November 18, 1996...

SWORN AND SUBSCRIBED TO BEFORE ME THIS

18th DAY OF November, 19 96

SIGNATURE

LT. John _____

THIS AFFIDAVIT TAKEN PURSUANT TO CHAPTER 18 OF THE LAWS OF 1953

Date: November 18, 1996
4 pages

Investigator Tim Braun wrote this report.

Investigator Braun told Dr. Natarajahn that Rashad confessed to the shooting and informed him of Rashad's account of the incident.

Forensic findings of Dr. Shaikah and Dr. Natarajahn contradict Rashad's version of the shooting.

Rashad claims he was some distance (3 feet) from Yaki at time of shooting.

Due to amount of stippling surrounding the wounds the forensic findings are that Yaki was shot at close range.

Rashad stated that Yaki was standing upright with Kaseem standing behind him. The Essex County Prosecutor's Office Report notes that Yaki was 6'4" and weighed 203 pounds, and that Clarke was 5'6"and weighed approximately 135 pounds.

Investigation continuing.

CONTINUATION REPORT

Supervisor Approval

Prosecuting Attorney 11/22/96

Section	Submitted by	Date	Section #
HOMICIDE	INV. TIM BRAUN	11-18-96	H#122-96

TO: LT. JOHN ARNOLD

RE: CONTINUED INVESTIGATION H#122-96

SIR:

DECEDENT: YAFEU FULA B/M/19YRS.
DEFENDANTS: NADIR WAY B/M/16YRS.
            RASHAD CLARKE B/M/17YRS.

FRIDAY NOVEMBER 15,1996

ON THIS DATE A BRIEFING WAS HELD AT THE HOMICIDE SQUAD WHERE THE
STATUS OF THIS INVESTIGATION WAS REVIEWED.   FOLLOWING THE
BRIEFING THE INVESTIGATION CONTINUED.

AT APPROXIMATELY 2:00PM THIS WRITER RESPONDED TO THE STATE MEDICAL
EXAMINERS OFFICE TO REVIEW THE RESULTS OF THE POSTMORTEM
EXAMINATION OF THE DECEDENT.   UPON MY ARRIVAL I REVIEWED THE
R.I.M.E. REPORT WHICH WAS SUBMITTED BY THE MEDICAL EXAMINERS
INVESTIGATORS MARILYN STINES & MAUREEN GARDNER.

DUE TO THE UNAVAILABILITY OF DR. JUNAID SHAIKH, I WAS ABLE TO SPEAK
WITH DR. GEETAH NATARAJAHN AFTER WHICH WE REVIEWED THE CASE FILE
(M.E.#07-96-2301).   PHOTOS WHICH WERE TAKEN BY THE MEDICAL
EXAMINERS STAFF WERE ALSO REVIEWED, AND DEPICTED THE DECEDENTS
WOUNDS AND HOW THEY APPEARED.   I ALSO ADVISED DR. NATARAJAHN THAT

1

THE SUSPECT (RASHAD CALRKE) HAD CONFESSED TO SHOOTING THE DECEDENT
AND HIS ACCOUNT OF HOW HE SHOT THE DECEDENT.

AFTER REVIEWING THE FORENSIC FINDINGS OF DR. SHAIKAH AND REVIEWING
THE PHOTOS, DR. NATARAJAHNS OPINION OF HOW THE DECEDENT WAS SHOT
DIFFERED FROM THAT OF RASHAAD CLARKES VERSION.   ACCORDING TO
CLARKE HE CLAIMS THAT HE WAS SOME DISTANCE FROM THE DECEDENT WHEN
HE ACCIDENTALLY SHOT THE DECEDENT.   DUE TO THE AMOUNT OF
STIPPLING SURROUNDING THE WOUND TO THE DECEDENTS RIGHT EYE IT WAS
APPARENT THAT THE DECEDENT WAS SHOT AT CLOSE RANGE.   THE
FORENSIC FINDINGS CLEARLY CONTRADICTED THE ACCOUNT OF RASHAAD
CLARKE, WHEN HE STATED THAT THE WEAPON HE USED TO SHOOT THE
DECEDENT WAS APPROXIMATELY 3 FEET AWAY FROM DECEDENT WHEN HE WAS
SHOT.

THE DEFENDANT (CLARKE) ALSO STATED THAT THE DECEDENT WAS STANDING
UPRIGHT AT THE TIME HE WAS SHOT WITH THE SECOND DEFENDANT (WAY)
STANDING BEHIND THE DECEDENT.   IT SHOULD BE NOTED THAT THE
DECEDENT IS 6'4" AND WEIGHED 203LBS. AT THE TIME OF HIS DEATH.   AT
THE TIME OF HIS ARREST CLARKE APPEARED TO BE 5'6" AND WEIGHED
APPROXIMATELY 135LBS., AND CLAIMS TO BE RIGHT HANDED, THE SAME HAND
HE HELD THE MURDER WEAPON AT THE TIME THE DECEDENT WAS SHOT.
THE POSITIONS OF ALL THREE WERE DESCRIBED AS THE DECEDENT AND
CLARKE STANDING FACE TO FACE WITH A AN UNKNOWN DISTANCE BETWEEN
THEM AND WAY STANDING DIRECTLY BEHIND THE DECEDENT.

FOLLOWING MY CONFERENCE WITH DR. NATARAJAHN I RETURNED TO THE
HOMICIDE SQUAD WHERE I ADVISED INV. JOHNSON OF THE MEDICAL
EXAMINERS FINDINGS.   I ALSO ADVISED INV. JOHNSON OF THE CONFLICT
BETWEEN THE FORENSIC EVIDENCE AND CLARKES ACCOUNT OF THE SHOOTING.

LATER THIS DATE I RESPONDED TO THE IRVINGTON CAB COMPANY 172 COIT
STREET IRIVINGTON,NJ.   AT THIS LOCATION I RETRIEVED THE ORIGINAL
DISPATCH LOG SHEET FOR THE TIMES IN QUESTION ON 11-10-96.   THE LOG
CLEARLY INDICATES A FARE ORIGINATING FROM 23 NADEN PL. TO ORANGE
BETWEEN 2:50AM - 3:15AM.   THE LOG IS A LETTER SIZE YELLOW LINED
PIECE OF PAPER WITH DISPATCH ENTRIES ON BOTH SIDES.   THE LOG SHEET
WAS OBTAINED FROM THE EVENING MANAGER ROBERT DALTON, WHO SIGNED THE
DOCUMENT IN MY PRESENCE TO SHOW THE CHAIN OF CUSTODY.   THIS
DOCUMENT WAS RETURNED TO THE HOMICIDE SQUAD AND LOGGED INTO
EVIDENCE BY THIS WRITER.

AT APPROXIMATELY 10:00PM THIS SAME DATE INV. MARK STOLARZ AND I

RESPONDED TO 92 SANFORD STREET EAST ORANGE, N.J. AT THIS ONE FAMILY HOME I SPOKE WITH MR. SAM ROGERS WHO IS KNOWN BY ME FROM A PREVIOUS INVESTIGATION. ACCORDING TO MR. ROGERS, IN THE EARLY MORNING HOURS OF SUNDAY NOVEMBER 10,1996 HE AND HIS FAMILY WERE ASLEEP WHEN HE WAS AWAKEN BY THE RINGING OF HIS DOORBELL BETWEEN 3:30AM-4:00AM. HE WENT TO THE WINDOW OF HIS SECOND FLOOR BEDROOM AND NOTICED IT WAS HIS NEPHEW (RASHAAD CLARKE), AFTER WHICH HE WENT DOWNSTAIRS AND ALLOWED HIM INTO HIS HOME.

ONCE HE OPENED THE DOOR MR. ROGERS NOTICED HIS NEPHEW WAS ALSO IN THE COMPANY OF ANOTHER YOUNG BLACK MALE KNOWN TO HIM AS KASSEM. AT THIS POINT MR. ROGERS ALLOWED BOTH YOUNG MEN INTO HIS HOME AND ASKED THEM IF THEY WISHED TO SPEND THE NIGHT. RASHAAD CLARKE ADVISED MR. ROGERS THAT HE HAD AN ARGUMENT WITH HIS BABY'S MOTHER AND HE HAD LEFT HER HOME. RASHAAD CLARKE THEN WENT TO THE KITCHEN AND CALLED FOR A TAXI TO TAKE HE AND KASSEM HOME TO IRVINGTON. THE TAXI ARRIVED APPROXIMATELY 10 MINUTES LATER AND THE TWO YOUNG MEN LEFT IN A GREEN COLOR TAXI CAB.

ACCORDING TO MR. ROGERS THE RELATIONSHIP BETWEEN HE AND CLARKE IS THAT HIS WIFE JUNE (CLARKE) ROGERS IS THE SISTER OF RASHAAD CLARKES DECEASED MOTHER GALINDA CLARKE. MR. ROGERS ALSO STATED THAT CLARKES FRIEND KASSEM, HAD BEEN AT HIS 92 SANFORD ST. HOME ON SEVERAL OCCASIONS PRIOR TO 11-10-96 WHILE HE WAS IN THE COMPANY OF CLARKE. MR. ROGERS HAS AGREED TO RESPOND TO THE HOMICIDE SQUAD ON 11-16-96 TO PROVIDE ME WITH A SWORN STATEMENT OUTLINING THE 11-10-96 VISIT OF CLARKE AND WAY. THE TOTAL TIME OF CLARKE & WAY STAYING AT MR. ROGERS HOME WAS APPROXIMATELY 15-20 MINUTES, DURING WHICH TIME MR. ROGERS WAS UNAWARE OF THE SHOOTING INCIDENT.

SATURDAY NOVEMBER 16,1996

ON THIS DATE MR. SAMUEL ROGERS WAS BROUGHT TO THE HOMICIDE SQUAD WHERE HE SUPPLIED A SWORN STATEMENT TO THIS WRITER PERTAINING TO CLARKE & WAY ARRIVING AT HIS HOME SHORTLY AFTER THE SHOOTING OF THE DECEDENT (SEE STATEMENT FOR DETAILS).

ALSO ON THIS DATE I RESPONDED TO THE HOME SAMIRA TURNER 27 WILSON PLACE IRVINGTON, NJ. UPON MY ARRIVAL AT APPROXIMATELY 3:00PM I FOUND THAT MS. TURNER WAS NOT AT HOME. A MESSAGE WAS LEFT WITH A MALE COUSIN WHO IDENTIFIED HIMSELF ONLY AS KAREEM, TO HAVE MS. TURNER CONTACT ME AS SOON AS POSSIBLE. ACCORDING TO A STATEMENT BY CLARKE, MS. TURNER IS HIS CURRENT GIRLFRIEND AND IT IS BELIEVED

3

THAT DUE TO THIS RELATIONSHIP SHE MAY HAVE KNOWLEDGE OF THIS INCIDENT. THEREFORE THE NEED TO INTERVIEW MS. TURNER IS ESSENTIAL.

LATER THIS SAME DATE I RESPONDED TO WESLAND TAXI COMPANY MAIN STREET E. ORANGE, NJ. IN AN ATTEMPT TO RETRIEVE THE ORIGINAL DISPATCH LOG SHEET FOR 11-10-96 I WAS MET WITH NEGATIVE RESULTS AT THIS TIME, DUE TO THE OFFICE BEING CLOSED AND A LANGUAGE BARRIER WITH THE STAFF WHO SPOKE LITTLE ENGLISH.

MONDAY NOVEMBER 18, 1996

ON THIS DATE I RESPONDED TO THE ORANGE POLICE DEPARTMENT TO RETRIEVE THE PROJECTILE RECOVERED FROM THE DECEDENT AT THE TIME OF HIS AUTOPSY. THE SAME PROJECTILE WAS THEN TRANSPORTED TO THE ESSEX CO. SHERIFF'S DEPARTMENT BALLISTICS LAB FOR FORENSIC TESTING. THE PROJECTILE WAS OBTAINED FROM ORANGE POLICE DETECTIVE JEROME ANDERSON AND TURNED OVER TO DETECTIVE GARY MAYER OF THE SHERIFF'S DEPARTMENT.

AFTER TRANSPORTING THE PROJECTILE TO THE SHERIFF'S DEPARTMENT IT WAS EXAMINED BY DET. MAYER AND ENTERED INTO THE I.B.I.S. (INTERGRATED BALLISTICS IDENTIFIICATION SYSTEM) FOR FUTURE COMPARISONS. THE PROJECTILE WAS CLASSIFIED AS A 38 CALIBER - 357 CALIBER CLASS LEAD WAD CUTTER WITH 6 LANDS AND 6 GROOVES WITH A LEFT TWIST.

INVESTIGATION CONTINUING:

RESPECTFULLY SUBMITTED,

INV. TIM BRAUN/HOMICIDE SQ.

THIS PAGE INTENTIONALLY LEFT BLANK

VOLUNTARY STATEMENT OF BRENDA TURNER

Date: November 19, 1996

5 pages

Redactions within statement made by publisher to protect personal information. Handwritten notes from providing agency; handwritten corrections by Brenda Turner.

Brenda Turner is the mother of Sameerah Turner, who is the mother of Rashad Clark's daughter.

Brenda states her daughter (Sameerah) said Rashad told her he threw the gun used to shoot Yaki in the sewer and Sameerah stated Rashad said the gunpowder was all over him. He went to different people's houses to get other clothing.

She states her daughter started getting money from Rashad's family after the shooting. Prior to that, she states Rashad's family didn't care about her daughter.

She states Sameerah told her Rashad told her he shot his friend.

Her daughter told her Rashad's charges were going to be dropped down to assault and he would be tried as a juvenile and would only get a year.

She states nobody called her daughter except Rashad called collect. Everyone from his family stopped calling after she came to the prosecutor's office to give her statement.

DATE	TIME	PLACE	
11/19/96	2219 hrs.	ESSEX COUNTY PROSECUTOR'S OFFICE	FILE NO HOM122-96

VOLUNTARY STATEMENT OF:	AGE
Brenda Turner	40 yrs. old

RESIDENCE	
27 Wilson Place, 2nd floor, Irvington	PHONE 372-

OCCUPATION	EMPLOYER
Emergency Med. Tech.	University Hospital

STATEMENT MADE TO
Inv. Howard Johnson Essex County Prosecutor's Office

I am Investigator Howard Johnson of the Essex County Prosecutor's Office. I would like to ask you some questions regarding events surrounding the shooting death of Yafeu A. Fula.

Q. Would you answer my questions?
A. Yes.

Q. What is your date of birth, and your social security number?
A. January 27, 1957.

Q. Can you read, write, and understand the English language?
A. Yes.

Q. How long have you lived at your current residence?
A. About eleven months. It will be a year in January. It's really ten months.

Q. Where did you live prior to your current address?
A. 248 Munn Avenue, Irvington.

Q. How long did you live at your previous address?
A. About a year.

Q. Where did you live prior to 248 Munn Avenue?
A. I believe it was across the street. Before that I lived in East Orange.

Q. Who lives with you at your current residence?
A. My two sons, Odarius Turner, Ezekiel Dixon, my three daughters, Jameelah Turner, Takila Holmes, Sameerah Turner, my nephew Kareem Turner, and my grand daughter, Shamtel Turner.

Q. What was the last formal school that you attended?
A. Umm, Essex County College.

Q. Do you know someone named Rashad Clark?
A. Yes.

Q. How do you know Rashad?
A. Through my daughter.

Q. Which daughter are you talking about, and what is their relationship?
A. Sameerah Turner. She had a baby by Rashad.

Q. What is Rashad's child's name?
A. Shantel Sateerah Turner.

Q. How old is Shantel?

SWORN AND SUBSCRIBED TO BEFORE ME THIS

20 DAY OF NOV 96

SIGNATURE

THIS AFFIDAVIT TAKEN PURSUANT TO CHAPTER 39 OF THE LAWS OF 1953

DATE 11/19/96	TIME 2219 hrs.	PLACE ESSEX COUNTY PROSECUTOR'S OFFICE	FILE NO. HOM122-96

VOLUNTARY STATEMENT OF Brenda Turner	AGE 40 yrs. old

RESIDENCE 27 Wilson Place, 2nd floor, Irvington	PHONE 372-

OCCUPATION Emergency Med. Tech.	EMPLOYER University Hospital

STATEMENT MADE TO
Inv. Howard Johnson   Essex County Prosecutor's Office

A. Three months.

Q. Do you know how long Sameerah, and Rashad have been seeing each other?
A. Oh, I didn't know about him until Sameerah was about three, or three and a half months pregnant. That was the first time that I met him.

Q. Do you know how Rashad supports his daughter?
A. Rashad gets social security from both of his deceased parents. Rashad doesn't support his daughter, I pay one hundred dollars for her to go to the doctors. Sometimes he buys Pampers.

Q. What are the circumstances of your daughter Sameerah being missing early last week?
A. She left out to go to night school, at about 4:30 p.m., Tuesday. She had to be at school at 5:00 p.m. She didn't return to home from Tuesday night, until Thursday about 1:30 in the afternoon. I was talking to Noel, when Sameerah telephoned on Thursday. Umm, Sameerah told me to get the baby ready, she was coming to get her baby, and she would tell me what happened when she got home. When she arrived home she said that, "Roddy killed somebody, and then she said that it was a accident". She that Roddy's lawyer was at his house, and he was supposed to turn himself in, but before he turned himself in he wanted to see all of his kids, and his niece. While Sameerah was upstairs in our house Rashad's aunt was sitting downstairs in her car, I think it's a '96 Neon, with her little daughter. I think she's about seven, or eight. Meanwhile, after Sameerah did leave, Rashad called me, and asked me did Sameerah get home yet? Then I started asking him questions. I asked him, do you know that Noonie haven't been home in two days, and I have her baby? He said yes. I said, Noonie said that you shot somebody, and he said yeah it was a accident, they was playing a gun, and the gun went off, and shot his friend in the face. So I said well maybe he didn't die. Rashad said, after it happened we ran out, and the people came out. He said that the boy's wake was Thursday, the same day that we were talking. I said that if they were going to have his wake on Thursday, it must have happened awhile ago. He said that it happened on Saturday.

Q. What is the driver's name of the '96 Neon?
A. I believe her name is Jameelah. Her car was white. My daughter Jameelah drives my car, and it's a '96 green Neon. I think that I had my care first, then they got theirs.

Q. Who is Noonie?
A. My sixteen year old daughter Sameerah.

Q. Did Roddy tell you that he had a gun?
A. Ummm, no. This is the first time that I knew that he had a gun. I think that he has been through this before.

Q. Is it unusual for Roddy's aunt Jameelah to visit, or pick up Sameerah, and the baby?
A. She have done it before.

Q. Would you be able to recognize Jameelah, if you saw her again?
A. Yes.

Q. Has Rashad been seeing you daughter, Sameerah continually through their relationship?

SWORN AND SUBSCRIBED TO BEFORE ME THIS

20 DAY OF NOV 96   _Brenda Turner_
                        SIGNATURE

THIS AFFIDAVIT TAKEN PURSUANT TO CHAPTER 39 OF THE LAWS OF 1953

DATE	TIME	PLACE	
11/19/96	2219 hrs.	ESSEX COUNTY PROSECUTOR'S OFFICE	NEWARK, NJ

VOLUNTARY STATEMENT OF:	FILE NO:
Brenda Turner	HOM122-96

RESIDENCE:	AGE:
27 Wilson Place, 2nd floor, Irvington	40 yrs. old

OCCUPATION:	EMPLOYER:	PHONE:
Emergency Med. Tech.	University Hospital	372■

STATEMENT MADE TO:
Inv. Howard Johnson   Essex County Prosecutor's Office

A. No.

Q. When did they stop seeing each other, and when did the relationship start back up again?
A. O.K., first of all Roddy stated to me the he didn't go with Sameerah. He would help her with the baby, but she could go with whoever she want to, as long as they don't hurt his child. When Sameerah had the baby, after having it, she wasn't seeing Roddy to often, maybe once a week, and when she did call their, they would say that he wasn't there, or he was asleep. The other girl with Roddy's baby was there, and every time that Noonie went there, the other girl was there. About two months ago, maybe once or twice Roddy came by to pick up the baby. He would come to pick up the baby in a taxi, and after school, Sameerah would pick her up, and bring her home.

Q. Did you overhear any conversations between Roddy, and, or any of his family members regarding the shooting?
A. Umm huh, when ~~Roddy~~ Rashad (BT) on that Thursday, I don't know if it was his grandfather, or his uncle, I heard him say in the background, " get off this phone it might be tapped". Roddy was telling me about the shooting.

Q. What phone number did Rashad call, when you talked to him about the shooting?
A. 372-■■■, but my caller I.D. said anonymous. It wouldn't let me know where he was.

Q. Has the frequency of the telephone conversations, and visits from Rashad, and his family increased, or decreased during this past week?
A. Umm, they started up Thursday, Friday, Saturday, and Sunday, all of them his cousins, sister, aunts. Every time the phone rang it was for Noonie, and it was one of them, and they would be on a three way. Noonie would listen, while the two other parties would talk. They would converse, and she would listen, while they talked. Some of the time she would join in, but most of the time she would listen. I would get upset, and I would tell her to get off of that phone, and I would say that they are grown women, your getting to get involved into something you don't know about. They would get to the part when the phone rand, they wouldn't say nothing, they wanted her to answer, since Noonie came here yesterday, it all stopped. If you call Mr. Sabur, he's the principal of the Irvington alternative program.

Q. How do you know what the people were talking about on the telephone?
A. I don't know what they were saying on the telephone, but I would hear some of the things that Sameerah would say, and I knew it was his family.

Q. How did you know that it was Rashad's family that was on the telephone?
A. O.K., two ways. Sometime their names would come up on the caller I.D., or sometimes they put anonymous: They are the only ones that do that. So when I see anonymous, I know that it's them.

Q. Have you ever eavesdropped on Sameerah's conversations with Rashad, or his family?
A. One time when Rashad was arguing with Noonie when she was pregnant, and made her get off of the phone.

Q. Do you know where the gun is that Rashad used to shoot the man in Orange?
A. If I'm not mistaken, I believed that Sameerah said, when I asked, Rashad threw it in a sewer.

Q. Do you have any knowledge of what happened to Rashad's clothing that he wore the night of the shooting?

SWORN AND SUBSCRIBED TO BEFORE ME THIS

_20_ DAY OF _Nov_ _96_   _Brenda Turner_
                          SIGNATURE

THIS AFFIDAVIT TAKEN PURSUANT TO CHAPTER 39 OF THE LAWS OF 1953

DATE	TIME	PLACE	FILE NO.
11/19/96	2219 hrs.	ESSEX COUNTY PROSECUTOR'S OFFICE	HOM122-96

VOLUNTARY STATEMENT OF:
Brenda Turner

AGE: 40 yrs. old

RESIDENCE:
27 Wilson Place, 2nd floor, Irvington

PHONE: 372-

OCCUPATION:
Emergency Med. Tech.

EMPLOYER:
University Hospital

STATEMENT MADE TO:
Inv. Howard Johnson   Essex County Prosecutor's Office

A. Sameerah stated that Rashad said that the gunpowder was all over him, so he took everything off, and he went like to different peoples houses. I like he took off a shirt, and they gave him a shirt, and so on. Sameerah said that the police came to Rashad's house, and stated that they needed all of his clothing. Rashad's family asked Sameerah could she go get them, and she did get them.

Q. Did you accompany your daughter Sameerah to this Office on Monday evening, November 18, 1996, for her to render a sworn statement regarding the shooting?
A. Yes.

Q. Did you give me your consent to take the statement?
A. Yes.

Q. Does Sameerah work?
A. Not now, Roddy told her that she didn't need to work, he was going to give her twenty five dollars a week.
  [Rashad ⓖ]

Q. How recently was it that Roddy told Sameerah that she did not have to work?
A. Umm, after she got her first paycheck from her job at Roy Rogers in Livingston, it was the first Monday after the shooting. All this took place after the shooting. I saw a big change in Noonie. All that I know is that she got money today, like it was no problem.

Q. Do you know where she received the money from, and for what reason?
A. First Noonie asked me can I get Shantel's pictures out of the shop a couple of days ago, and I told her that I didn't have the money. So today she just came out and said, Rashad's brother is going to give me the forty dollars for the pictures. So this is when my daughter Jameelah rode over to Rashad's house, and Rashad's brother gave Sameerah twenty dollars, instead of forty, and then this evening Rashad was on the three way. Rashad called collect to his family member, I don't know it was his aunt, or his sister, and they called Noonie. Noonie asked, or told Rashad that she needed twenty more dollars, and Rashad told her to call on my three way, and they spoke to Rashad's grandfather, Mr. O. Rashad to Mr. O to give Noonie the twenty dollars.

Q. Did Mr. O give Noonie the twenty dollars?
A. I don't know as yet.

Q. Has the money, and the attention been constant towards Noonie, and Shantel?
A. No.

Q. How recent has it been since the Clark family has been so interested in the health, and well being of Sameerah, and Shantel?
A. They just started. They don't care. They on that other girls side. I told him that they don't care about her.

Q. Do you know who Lameesh is?
A. I don't know him. I just talked to him on the phone. He went to the movies with Noonie on Friday. Before Friday he was calling her all along. The last thing I heard from him was Friday. Sameerah said to me that Monday after the shooting that I'll just go back with Roddy.

SWORN AND SUBSCRIBED TO BEFORE ME THIS

20 DAY OF NOV , 19 96   _Brenda Turner_
SIGNATURE

Robert P. Carelli
THIS AFFIDAVIT TAKEN PURSUANT TO CHAPTER 39 OF THE LAWS OF 1953

DATE	TIME	PLACE	FILE NO.
11/19/96	2219 hrs.	ESSEX COUNTY PROSECUTOR'S OFFICE	HOM122-96

VOLUNTARY STATEMENT OF:
Brenda Turner

AGE:
40 yrs. old

RESIDENCE:
27 Wilson Place, 2nd floor, Irvington

PHONE:
372-

OCCUPATION:
Emergency Med. Tech.

EMPLOYER:
University Hospital

STATEMENT MADE TO:
Inv. Howard Johnson Essex County Prosecutor's Office

Q. Did you find out where Sameerah was when you called the Irvington Police Department?
A. No.

Q. Did you find out where she was at a later date?
A. Umm, I think that Sameerah was staying with Rashad at his aunt's house, because he said it that Thursday that he turned himself in. The Caller I.D. said anonymous, but Roddy said that he was at his aunt's.

Q. Did Sameerah tell you that Roddy shot his friend?
A. Umm huh, yes.

Q. Did Sameerah ever tell you whether someone was with Rashad, or was he alone?
A. She never said it, but Rashad that we ran, and when they said on the news that they got two boys.

Q. Did Sameerah ever tell you who paid for Rashad's lawyer?
A. Yes, She said that Rashad just got a three thousand dollar law suit, and his grandfather said that he was going to get Rashad a Public Defender, and Rashad's brother said don't get a Public defender they work for the police.

Q. Do you know how the family came about hiring their lawyer?
A. The same lawyer represented his brother, or his uncle, who ever it was just got out of jail. He told the lawyer that you owe me a favor.

Q. Do you know the name of the lawyer?
A. No. I asked her if he was Caucasian or black, and Noonie said that he was Caucasian. She said that Rashad's charges were going to be dropped down to assault, he would be tried as a juvenile, and if he got anything he would only get a year.

Q. Do you wish to add anything to your statement?   Rashad (BT)
A. Umm, no. That's it. Nobody called Sameerah today except ~~Roddy~~ called her collect. Everybody stopped calling after she came up to this office to give her statement. Now nobody's calling her now, where are all of her friends?

Q. Have any threats, or promises been made to you for you to render this statement?
A. No.

Q. Do you swear, or affirm that the information which you have just provided, is the whole truth, and you do so under penalty of the law?
A. Yes I do.

Q. At the conclusion of your statement, would you read it, make corrections, and when you are satisfied that it contains exactly what you have told me, would you sign it?
A. Yes.

Statement ended at ~~1257 hours on~~ November 20, 1996..
        0057 (BT)

SWORN AND SUBSCRIBED TO BEFORE ME THIS

20 DAY OF NOV 19 96   Brenda Turner
                                            SIGNATURE

THIS AFFIDAVIT TAKEN PURSUANT TO CHAPTER 39 OF THE LAWS OF 1953

CONTINUATION REPORT IN RE: CONFESSION OF RASHAD CLARK

Date: November 22, 1996
10 pages
Redactions, handwritten notes, and underlines made by providing agency.

Rashad gave a possible location of weapon he discarded when he fled scene although it was never found.

Rashad claims he had no misunderstandings or arguments with Yaki which contradicts Garfield Sharpe's statement who says he threatened to kill Yaki.

Rashad states he entered a cab and directed driver (Moinville Ovil) to proceed to the Mechanic Street Projects.

Rashad indicates he saw Kaseem Way and opened the cab door to call out to Kaseem. He states he did not want Kaseem to accompany him because he was going to see a female friend at Mechanic Street but Kaseem insisted on coming along. This contradicts driver Moinville Ovil's statement that he was directed to go to Chancelor and Union where a passenger was waiting.

Rashad states Yaki was standing approximately three feet away at the time of the shooting. This contradicts Essex County Prosecutor's Office Continuation Report and Dr. Geetah Natarajahn. Those reports indicate the amount of stippling surrounding the wound of Yaki's right eye show it was clear he was shot at close range and could not have been three feet away. That report also notes that Yaki was 6'4" and weighed 203 pounds, and that Rashad was 5'6"and weighed approximately 135 pounds. The forensic findings do not support Rashad's version of events.

Rashad admits to knowing Yaki had on a bulletproof vest.

Homicide investigation is ongoing.

Robert P. Carella
Supervisor's Approval

A. Taylor 12/2/96
Prosecuting Attorney

Section	Asst. Prosecutor/Detective	Date	Section #
Homicide	Inv. Arnold Valentin, Jr.	11/22/96	H# 122-96

TO: LIEUTENANT ROBERT P. CARELLA

RE: HOMICIDE INVESTIGATION # 122-96
DECEDENT: YAFEU A. FULA B/M, 19
DEFENDANT(S): NADIR WAY B/M, 17
               RASHAD CLARK B/M, 16

Date 2/16/98 GJ Clerk

STATE EXHIBIT # S-3

SIR:

On Thursday, November 14, 1996, the undersigned Investigator along with Orange Police Department Detective Jerome Anderson and Assistant Prosecutor Catherine Fantuzzi interviewed Mr. Rashad Lateef Clark. Mr. Clark was interviewed in the presence of his grandfather Erza Clark along with his attorney Richard Banas. The interview was in regards to the shooting death of Yafeu A. Fula, who was shot and killed on Sunday, November 10, 1996, at 325 Mechanic Street in Orange, New Jersey. Mr. Clark was read his Constitutional Rights via the Preamble to a signed statement form and indicated that he understood them as well as sign the form along with his attorney.

During the course of the preliminary interview, Mr. Clark admitted shooting the decedent and disclosed a possible location of the weapon used in the shooting. Mr. Clark stated that he had thrown the weapon in a drainage sewer several blocks away from 325 Street, after he fled the scene of the shooting. The interview was then interrupted at this juncture and arrangements were made for Mr. Clark and his attorney to join the undersigned along with members of the Prosecutor's Office and Orange Police Department, to search for the weapon in the area of 325 Mechanic Street. The search for the weapon was fruitless.

Mr. Clark identified himself as Rashad Lateef Clark also known as "Roddy". His date of birth is 12/06/79, and he did not know his social security number. Mr. Clark stated that he resides at 23 Naden Place in Irvington, New Jersey, with his grandfather Erza Clark, with a telephone number of (201) 375-2341. Mr. Clark stated that he could read and understand the English language, and that the last grade in school upon completion is the 10th grade at Irvington High School.

Mr. Clark was then requested to describe his relationship with the decedent and the last time they met prior to the shooting. Mr. Clark stated that he met with the decedent approximately a week before the shooting in the town of Montclair, New Jersey. The meeting was held on the street at the intersection of Bloomfield Avenue and New Street. Mr. Clark characterized his relationship with the decedent as "good friends" and that they have known each other over the past two and one-half years. Mr. Clark also knew the decedent as "Ya", "Kap", and "Kadafi". Their relationship centered around their mutual interest in music where the decedent was affiliated with the record label "Death Row".

Mr. Clark was specifically asked if he had any argument's or misunderstanding's with the decedent leading up to the time of the shooting. Mr. Clark replied he did not. Mr. Clark was then questioned as to being in possession of guns and his knowledge of the decedent in possession of guns. Mr. Clark replied that he frequently played with guns and that he had observed the decedent on prior occasions in possession of guns. Mr. Clark was then questioned if he or the decedent was affiliated with "gangs". Mr. Clark stated that he did not belong to a gang, although he just associated with friends on his block and that they were fighting with the boys from Colgate Park.

Mr. Clark was then requested to describe the events that transpired on Thursday, November 10, 1996, prior to the shooting. Mr. Clark stated that he was unclear about the time but states it was approximately after 12:00 o'clock midnight when he telephoned from his house the residence at 325 Mechanic Street in Orange, New Jersey asking for the decedent. Mr. Clark stated that he telephoned (201) 673-3617 and spoke with a women named "Talibah". "Talibah" was the cousin or sister of the decedent's girlfriend. Mr. Clark did not know the apartment number of the residence he called but described it's location as being on the third floor of the above address all the way down the hallway on the right. Mr. Clark asked "Talibah" on the phone if the decedent was there and she replied that he would soon be there and that it was alright for Mr. Clark to come over. Mr. Clark then stated that he proceeded to call two Taxi Cab companies; Irvington Cab Company and Red Cap Cab company contacted at (201) 373-5000 and (201) 371-5600 respectfully.

3

Mr. Clark stated that he utilizes these two Cab Companies frequently. Mr. Clark stated that the Irvington Cab Company arrived approximately 20-30 minutes after his conversation with "Talibah". Mr. Clark then stated that he attempted to contact "Talibah" once again by telephone but no one picked up the phone. Mr. Clark made this second attempt to contact "Talibah" in an effort to get her exact address. Mr. Clark was then asked if he was in possession of a gun when he left his residence. Mr. Clark replied, "no". Mr. Clark was then asked to describe the clothing that he wore when he left his residence. Mr. Clark stated that he was wearing a blue and black waist length zippered jacket with the wording "North Face" on the front and back of the jacket. He also wore blue jean pants and black and white Adidas sneakers, a red shirt and a red scully hat. He had in his possession approximately $30.00 to $40.00 dollars. Mr. Clark stated that he entered the Irvington Cab at his residence. Mr. Clark was requested to describe the cab driver and he replied that he could not. Mr. Clark then stated that he entered the cab and directed the driver to proceed to the Mechanic Street Projects located in Orange. The cab then came to a stop at the corner of Paine and Union Avenue in Irvington when he observed his friend Nadir Kaseem Way. Mr. Clark stated the he opened the cab door and proceeded to call out for Mr. Way as he ducked down inside of the cab. Mr. Way then made his way over to the cab and spoke with Mr. Clark. Mr. Way then asked Mr. Clark where he was going and Mr. Clark informed him. Mr. Clark revealed that he didn't want Mr. Way to accompany him because Mr. Clark had intentions of speaking with a female friend at the 325 Mechanic Street apartment and didn't want his friend to just wait

BUT HE AT FIRST STATE

HAT HE CAME OVER TO 325 MECH

4

around. Mr. Clark then stated that Mr. Way insisted on coming ✳
along and jumped into the cab with Mr. Clark. Mr. Clark was then
requested to describe his relationship with Mr. Way. Mr. Clark
stated that he has known Nadir Kassem Way for approximately eight
years and considered him a good friend. Mr. Clark was then asked
to describe Mr. Way's clothing and he specified that he only could
recall that Mr. Way was wearing a black jacket. Mr. Clark was then
asked if he observed Mr. Way with a gun and he replied that he did
not.

The cab then proceeded to the projects and stopped in front of
325 Mechanic Street. Mr. Clark then stated that he and Mr. Way
exited the cab while he payed $12.00 dollars and Mr. Way payed the
rest for the fare. Mr. Clark was asked if he requested the cab to
stay and he said he did not. Mr. Clark was asked what was his
conversation with Mr. Way inside of the cab. Mr. Clark replied
that he didn't recall but he did remember that they were smoking a
"blunt" (cigar filled with marijuana). Mr. Clark was then asked if
he knew what time they arrived at their location and if they spoke
with anyone upon entering the building. Mr. Clark replied that he
did not know what time they arrived and that they spoke with no one
when they entered the building. They went straight to the third
floor and knocked on Talibah's door. He had only been to this
location on two prior occasions. Mr. Clark stated that he
proceeded to knock on the door rather hard. A women opened the
door and he described only as being dark skinned, medium weight,
and hair down to her neck while unsure about her age. Directly
behind this women was the decedent. The decedent stepped forward

and yelled at Mr. Clark for knocking hard on his door. According to Mr. Clark, the decedent proceeded to throw a playful punch at Mr. Clark as the decedent walked into the hallway and closed the door behind him. Mr. Clark then stated that he and the decedent along with Mr. Way proceeded to walk down the hallway "hiking on each other (exchanging insults ect.). Mr. Clark then stated that he gave the decedent a "blunt" that he was smoking. The decedent then shared the "blunt" with Mr. Way. Mr. Clark was then asked to describe the decedent. He described him as a tall, thin, male wearing a black coat, black pants. and a blue or red sweater. The decedent then proceeded to pull out a "blunt" of his own and started smoking it. As the decedent held the "blunt" in his left hand, the decedent pulled out a gun with his right hand from an unknown location on his body according to Mr. Clark. Mr. Clark stated that the decedent told him to look at the gun and that Mr. Clark reached out and grabbed the gun with his right hand. Mr. Clark described the gun as a .38 caliber handgun, black in color with a short barrel. I asked Mr. Clark how did he know it was a .38 caliber handgun, he replied that he remember's reading it on the gun. Mr. Clark then stated that he didn't know whether the gun was loaded or not. He began inspecting the handgun by turning it from side to side. Mr . Clark was requested to indicate everyone's position in the hallway and he stated that the decedent was directly in front of him in a standing position with Mr. Way directly behind the decedent. Mr. Clark stated that his back was to the door that the decedent exited. Mr. Clark was then requested to stand up and use the tiles in the interview room as an example of distance away from the decedent as they stood in the hallway.

6

I indicated to Mr. Clark that the tiles were 18 inches wide. Mr. Clark demonstrated the distance between he and the decedent at the time of the shooting. Mr. Clark did so and the distance was measured off to two tiles. Therefore, Mr. Clark indicated that he was approximately three feet away from the decedent at the time of the shooting. Mr. Clark was then asked to describe the event's of the shooting. Mr. Clark stated that as the decedent stood across from him in an upright position he was looking down at the gun turning it from side to side with his finger in the trigger guard. According to Mr. Clark he knows he must of squeezed the trigger but does not recall doing so. The gun is then fired and he observes the body of the decedent "jolt". The body of the decedent then fell back into the arms of Mr. Way as the decedent's body dropped to the ground. Mr. Clark stated that after the shooting he grabbed his head and said, "Oh shit, damn, what the fuck I do". Mr. Clark stated that Mr. Way stated, "Oh shit, Roddy". Mr. Clark stated that he stepped away from the decedent, then walked towards the decedent and then Mr. Way stated running and Mr. Clark followed. Mr. Clark stated that he started running with the gun in his hand as he ran out of the building.

Pursuant to information obtained during this investigation, Mr. Clark was asked if he encountered a dog that bit him on the hand while he was in the hallway. He said he did not. The undersigned observed Mr. Clark's hands and did not observe any breaks in his skin.

Mr. Clark stated that he and Mr. Way made a left while exiting the building and running in an unknown direction dropping the gun in a sewer between Mechanic Street and Sanford Avenue in East

Orange. Mr. Clark stated that while running he ended up on Sanford Avenue in East Orange and proceeded to 96 Sanford Avenue. He knocked on the door and his Uncle Sammy opened the door. Mr. Clark asked for his aunt Betty but she was asleep. Mr. Clark then spoke with cousin "Talibah", and told her that he had shot the decedent. Mr. Clark described "Talibah" as being a light skinned female, tall, approximately 5'9", skinny, approximately 27 to 28 years old. Mr. Clark then stated that he asked his Uncle Sammy for the number of a East Orange cab company. Mr. Clark placed the call from the kitchen phone. While at "Talibah's" house he received a page on his beeper. The number on his page was his house. He telephoned his house and spoke either to his sister or his brother he did not recall. They clicked over to call waiting and Mr. Clark started speaking with a man called, Mutah Beale, who was calling from Atlanta, who informed him that the decedent had been shot. Mr. Clark stated that he did not disclose what had occurred and told them that he was on his way home. Mr. Clark then stated that the cab had arrived and that he and Mr. Way entered the cab and headed home. Mr. Clark stated that when he got home he went straight to sleep. The next morning when he got up he stated that he told his grandfather Erza Clark what he had done along with a women named Maxine Beale. Mr. Clark indicated to them that he had made a mistake.

Mr. Clark was then asked if he knew where he had shot the decedent. He stated that he saw blood coming from the decedent's right eye.

8

Mr. Clark was then asked if he knew that the decedent was wearing a bullet proof vest. He replied that he did know that the decedent had a bullet proof vest because the decedent showed him. Mr. Clark stated that the decedent always had a gun on him because he sold

Mr. Clark was then requested to turn over his pager. Mr. Clark stated that he had given the beeper to his baby's mother, Samira Turner, residing at 27 Wilson Place, Irvington, New Jersey, with a telephone number of (201) 372-1377.

Mr. Clark was then asked for the location of the clothes he wore during the shooting. Mr. Clark replied that the clothing was at home and he gave his verbal consent to obtain the clothing in the presence of his attorney.

Arrangement's were made with Mr. Clark's grandfather, Erza Clark, and the clothing was obtained on November 14, 1996, with a signed consent to search form by the Clark Family. For further details refer to the undersigned's continuation reports in the file)

Mr. Clark was then asked if he intended to kill the decedent? He stated,"no". He was asked if he intended to rob the decedent? He stated, "no". He was asked why he shot the decedent? He stated that it was an "accident". Mr. Clark then stated that he didn't mean to kill the decedent.

Mr. Clark was then asked if the decedent had disclosed any of the events that transpired during the "Tu-Pac Shakur murder investigation"? Mr. Clark replied that the decedent only stated that it was "fucked up" that he was killed.

Mr. Clark was asked if he had ever met Tu-Pac Shakur? Mr. Clark replied that he had met him once at the past MTV awards in New York City.

Mr. Clark was then asked if all that was stated in the interview was the truth? He stated, "yes".

This is an ongoing homicide investigation.

Respectfully submitted,

Arnold Valentin, Jr.
County Investigator
Homicide Squad

THIS PAGE INTENTIONALLY LEFT BLANK

ESSEX CO. PROSECUTOR'S OFFICE
PLEA OFFER

Dated: various
1 page

Date plea tendered is 6/30/98.

Defendant agrees to a guilty plea for Manslaughter 2 and Unlawful Possession of a Weapon 3.

Rashad acknowledges shooting Yaki while handling a gun.

Rashad states co-defendant Nadir Way "was there fooling around wrestling with victim." In the statement from Lavie Johnson, she says she called Rashad's home looking for him after the shooting. She states his brother Sharif answered the phone. Sharif told Lavie that Rashad says Nadir had Yaki in a chokehold when Rashad shot him.

ESSEX COUNTY PROSECUTOR'S OFFICE REQUEST TO RECOMMEND DISPOSITION

PATRICIA A. HURT, ESSEX COUNTY PROSECUTOR   PATRICK P. TOSCANO, JR., FIRST ASSISTANT PROSECUTOR

RASHAD CLARKE
_____
Defendant

Reciprocal Discovery Received: _____ XX
                                    Yes   No

98-02-00698   11-10-96
_____   _____
Indictment/Accusation Number   (D/I)

_____   _____
Indictment/Accusation Number   (D/I)

P98001004/Homicide #122-96
_____
"P" Number/Homicide Number   Forfeiture File No.

_____
"P" Number/Homicide Number   Forfeiture File No.

Charges:
1 - MURDER 1°

2 - UNL POSS WEAPON 3°

3 - POSS WEAPON FOR UNL PURPOSE 2°

Charges:

The defendant is __18__ years old with: ___0___ prior indictable convictions; ___0___ prior D.P. convictions; and __4__ prior juvenile adjudications. The defendant is charged together with __one__ co-defendants.

The charges against the defendant involve the operation of: The Graves Act, __yes__; Prior conviction of PWI/Distribution CDS __no__; The Three Strike Act, __no__; The N.J. No Early Release Act, __no__ (In cases involving the No Early Release Act, the defendant must serve 85% of the sentence imposed by the court and face a period of 5 years parole supervision for a first degree offense; 3 years for a second degree offense.)
The defendant agrees to retract his/her prior plea of not guilty and enter a plea of guilty to the following charges: _____

Ct 1 as amended to Manslaughter 2°; ct 2 Unl Poss Weapon 3°

The defendant agrees to relinquish all rights to ___not applicable___ the subject of a pending forfeiture action and sign a consent order/judgment to that effect prior to sentence. The defendant agrees to make restitution to the victim(s) in the amount of _____ or as ordered by the court.

After sentencing, the State will move to dismiss the following charges: Ct 3 Poss Weapon for Unl Purpose 2°

At time of sentencing, the State will recommend that any custodial sentence not exceed: __10 years with a 5 year__

__period of parole ineligibility pursuant to the Graves Act__
The State reserves the right to be heard at sentencing and the right to retract the plea offer if the defendant fails to provide a truthful factual basis under oath; is arrested for another offense pending sentence; fails to appear at time of sentence; fails to comply with any condition of the plea offer or any order of the court. This offer constitutes the entire agreement between the parties notwithstanding the existence of other open charges against the defendant.

_____, Assistant Prosecutor
C. Brian Kapalin

June 22, 1998
Date of Plea Offer

APPROVED

Request to Recommend Disposition approved by:

APPROVED

6/26/98
Patricia A. Hurt, Essex County Prosecutor

6/26/98
Patrick P. Toscano, Jr.
First Assistant Prosecutor

6/22/98
Joseph P. Donohue, Sara S. McArdle, Norman Menz,
Charlotte Smith, Siobhan A. Teare, D F A P's

Glenn D. Goldberg, C A P
Michael White, C.A.P.

Steven Farman, Paul Bradley,
Robert Laurino, A.P. / Dirs

Eileen Cosgrove, A.P. / Supv.

Brian Kapalin, A.P./ Supv.
Thomas McTigue, A.P./ Supv.

Date plea tendered 6-30-98 Judge CAMP Defense Attorney R DAVIS Accepted X Rejected ____

Plea Cutoff: _____ Sentence Date: 9-11-98 Factual Basis △ ACKNOWLEDGE SHOOTING THE VICTIM WHILE HE WAS HANDLING THE GUN. HE SAID THAT NOOX WAY WAS THERE FOOLING AROUND WRESTLING WITH VICTIM.

EPILOGUE

On Thursday, November 14, 1996, Yafeu "Yaki Kadafi" Fula was laid to rest. The services held at Martin's Funeral Home in Montclair, NJ were filled to capacity by the young people who gathered in long lines to say good-bye to Yaki. He was 19 years old.

At the time of the killing, Rashad Clark was 16 years old. In 1998, the murder charge was reduced to manslaughter – against the wishes of his mother Yaasmyn Fula. He pled to manslaughter and was sentenced in September 1998, almost two years after the homicide of Yaki.

Prior to the sentencing in September 1998, Rashad was not in custody and during that time, he was charged with various crimes, including manufacture or distribution of controlled dangerous substances and a second charge at that same time for doing it on/near a school property or school bus.

After his release for the homicide, by 2006, Rashad returned to New Jersey and continued to rack up charges for use, possession, and distribution of controlled dangerous substances, assault, forgery, and various motor vehicle infractions.

In October 2014, he was the Most Wanted Fugitive of the Week for Hunterdon County, NJ.

On December 7, 2017, per a press release from the US Attorney's Office of the Eastern District of Virginia titled, ***"King of Death" Supplier Pleads Guilty to Heroin and Fentanyl Charges,*** Rashad pled guilty to a charge of conspiracy to manufacture, distribute and possess with intent to manufacture and distribute heroin, fentanyl, and furanylfentanyl resulting in death, in violation of 21 U.S.C. §§ 846 and 813.

Court documents say Rashad supplied Erskine Dawson Jr. with heroin and fentanyl from September to December 2016. Rashad hid thousands of wax baggies filled with heroin and fentanyl in stuffed animals and trafficked them from New Jersey to Virginia, where he would stay to oversee Dawson's operation.

On April 2, 2018, the television station WTKR reported Rashad was sentenced to 37 years behind bars for supplying a drug dealer with heroin and fentanyl known as "King of Death," and said his drugs were linked to overdoses and deaths of users in Hampton Roads in 2016.

WTKR went on to report that the DEA in partnership with officers from the Virginia Beach and Chesapeake police departments executed the search warrants, made arrests, and seized guns and over 1,800 baggies of heroin and fentanyl.

A court document was filed during the sentencing by Rashad through his counsel, showing Rashad entered a guilty plea prior to trial for the distribution of heroin and fentanyl. The request by counsel to receive only the minimum sentence of 240 months was rejected by the Judge.

Sentencing was before District Judge Raymond A. Jackson, held on April 2, 2018.

Imprisonment: Four Hundred Forty-Four (444) Months;
Supervised Release: Five (5) Years;
Special Assessment: $100.00

We decreed to the Children of Israel that if anyone kills a person—unless in retribution for murder or spreading corruption in the land—it is as if he kills all mankind, while if any saves a life it is as if he saves the lives of all mankind.

~Qur'an 5:32
Translated by M.A.S. Abdel Haleem,
King Fahd Professor of Islamic Studies,
University of London

SOURCES

The scanned documents within this book were provided directly to Yaasmyn Fula as part of the Crime Victims Bill of Rights for the State of New Jersey.

Other sources:

- Butterfield, Fox (1995) *All God's Children: The Bosket Family and the American Tradition of Violence*
- Haleem, M.A.S. Abdel (2008) *The Qur'an*
- Justice.gov, the Federal website for the Department of Justice
- The Newark Public Library newspaper archive
- NJcourts.gov, online database that includes court records for the State of New Jersey
- Pacer.gov, the online Federal database of court cases
- WTKR, a CBS network affiliate based in Norfolk, VA